Ernest Hemingway

The Short Happy Life of Francis Macomber

and Other Stories

Model Interpretations
by Detlev Gohrbandt

Ernst Klett Verlag

Lehrerbuch von Dr. Detlev Gohrbandt, Saarbrücken

The stories to which these interpretations refer are also available in a students' edition: *The Short Happy Life of Francis Macomber and Other Stories* (Klettbuch 57738).

Illustration acknowledgments: Interfoto, München: inside cover; Mary Hemingway (Family Collection) and Charles Scribner's Sons: pp. 18, 76, 105; Ernst Friedrich, *Krieg dem Kriege!* Berlin: Freie Jugend 1924: p. 75; Lawrence T. Barnett: p. 33.

ISBN 3-12-577390-3

1. Auflage 1 5 4 3 2 1 | 1989 88 87 86 85

Die letzte Zahl bezeichnet das Jahr dieses Druckes.

Umschlaggestaltung: Hans Lämmle, Stuttgart.
Druck: Gutmann & Co., Heilbronn. Printed in Germany.

Contents

Introduction
Biographical Note 6
The Craft of Fiction 7

Introduction to the Teacher's Book
The Texts 10
The Ice-Berg Theory 10
The Simple Style 12
Nick Adams 15
Introductory Lesson 17

Part I
The End of Something 19

Interpretation and Teaching Notes
Background 23
In Our Time 23
Structure 24
First Unit: Action, Scene and Symbol 26
Second Unit: Knowing and Saying 28
Third Unit: Plot and Ending 29
For Further Study 31
Additional Vocabulary 31

Part II
The Age Demanded (a poem by Ernest Hemingway) 33
Soldier's Home 34
Bombardment (a poem by Richard Aldington) 41

Interpretation and Teaching Notes
Background 42
Analysis 43
The Poems 47
First Unit: Back Home 48
Second Unit: Reconstituting the Dialogues 51
Third Unit: The Disharmony of Roles and Standards 54
For Further Study 57

Part III
Today Is Friday 60
Roman Wall Blues (a poem by W. H. Auden) 64

Interpretation and Teaching Notes
Background 65
Analysis 65
First Unit: Points of View 71
Second Unit: The Meaning of the Experience 72
For Further Study 73

Part IV
A Vignette from *In Our Time* 76
A Way You'll Never Be 77
Shell-shock (from *Everyman's Encyclopaedia*) 88

Interpretation and Teaching Notes
Background 89
Supplementary Texts 90
Analysis 91
First Unit: Action Past and Present 95
Second Unit: A Portrait of War 97
Third Unit: Make-believe or Truth? 99
Fourth Unit: A Way I'll Never Be? 100
For Further Study 101
Additional Vocabulary 103

Part V
The Short Happy Life of Francis Macomber 105
Shootism versus Sport: The Second Tanganyika Letter 134

Interpretation and Teaching Notes
Background 138
Analysis 139
The Hero and the Code 146
Supplementary Text 148
First Unit: Finding Out What Happened 149
Second Unit: Why It Happened That Way 151
Third Unit: Macomber's Conversion 154
Fourth Unit: The Relation of Saying and Doing 157

Fifth Unit: The Hero and the Code 160
For Further Study 162
Additional Vocabulary 164

INTRODUCTION

Biographical Note

The stories in this volume were all written in the first half of Ernest Hemingway's career, in the twenties and thirties. The following summary is by way of an introduction to his life and work from 1899 to 1936.

1899	Birth of Ernest Hemingway on July 21, in Oak Park, Illinois.
1917	The United States enters World War I. Hemingway works as a reporter on the Kansas City *Star.*
1918	Hemingway volunteers as a Red Cross ambulance driver in Italy and is wounded near Fossalta di Piave on July 8. In hospital, he falls in love with an American nurse, Agnes von Kurowsky.
1919	He returns home, feels lonely and homesick for Italy. "When [his sister] Marcelline came home on weekends, she thought he resembled someone 'put in a box with the cover nailed down.'" (Carlos Baker, *Ernest Hemingway. A Life Story*, p. 57)
1920–24	He works for the Toronto *Star* and *Star Weekly* papers.
1921	His first marriage, to Hadley Richardson. They move to Paris, where Hemingway works as a war correspondent in the Graeco-Turkish War of 1921–22.
1925	*In Our Time* is published (including "Soldier's Home", "The End of Something" and the interchapter "While the bombardment . . .").
1927	His second book of short stories, *Men Without Women*, appears (containing "Today Is Friday").
1931	Hemingway, with his second wife Pauline, moves to Key West, Florida. Here he can pursue his hobby of fishing.
1933	*Winner Take Nothing*, the third collection of short stories, is published (containing "A Way You'll Never Be"). In December 1933 Ernest, Pauline and two friends arrive in Kenya. They hire the white hunter Philip Percival as their guide. The safari experiences go into the writing of *Green Hills of Africa* (1935) and "The Short Happy Life of Francis Macomber".

5

The Craft of Fiction

A contemporary view of Hemingway is given by a leading figure of literary Paris between the wars, Gertrude Stein, in her autobiography.

So Hemingway was twenty-three, rather foreign looking, with passionately interested, rather than interesting eyes. He sat in front of Gertrude Stein and listened and looked.

They talked then, and more and more, a great deal together. He asked her to come and spend an evening in their apartment and look at his work. Hemingway had then and has always a very good instinct for finding apartments in strange but pleasing localities and good femmes de ménage and good food. This his first apartment was just off the place du Tertre. We spent the evening there and he and Gertrude Stein went over all the writing he had done up to that time. He had begun the novel that it was inevitable he would begin and there were the little poems afterwards printed by McAlmon in the Contact Edition. Gertrude Stein rather liked the poems, they were direct, Kiplingesque, but the novel she found wanting. There is a great deal of description in this, she said, and not particularly good description. Begin over again and concentrate, she said.

Hemingway was at this time Paris correspondent for a canadian newspaper. He was obliged there to express what he called the canadian viewpoint.

He and Gertrude Stein used to walk together and talk together a great deal. One day she said to him, look here, you say you and your wife have a little money between you. Is it enough to live on if you live quietly. Yes, he said. Well, she said, then do it. If you keep on doing newspaper work you will never see things, you will only see words and that will not do, that is of course if you intend to be a writer. Hemingway said he undoubtedly intended to be a writer. [. . .]

After that they met quite often. Gertrude Stein always says she likes to see him, he is so wonderful. And if he could only tell his own story. [. . .]

Hemingway [. . .] said once, I turn my flame which is a small one down and down and then suddenly there is a big explosion. If there were nothing but explosions my work would be so exciting nobody could bear it.

From *The Autobiography of Alice B. Toklas* by Gertrude Stein (1933), New York: Vintage Books, 1955, pp. 212–213, 220.

7 **femme(s) de ménage** *French:* housekeeper(s)

6

The following is an extract from Carlos Baker's biography of Ernest Hemingway. Carlos Baker got to know Hemingway in the fifties.

When they moved in on January 9, 1922, Ernest wrote his friends that they were living in "the best part of the Latin Quarter."

For the first time since the winter in Petoskey, he was free to write as he chose. He was determined to begin afresh with brand-new standards of truth and simplicity. "All you have to do is write one true sentence," he told himself. "Write the truest sentence that you know." It must be above all a "true simple declarative sentence" without scrollwork or ornamental language of any sort. It must deal with something he knew from personal experience. Stories like "The Passing of Pickles McCarty" or "Wolves and Doughnuts" had been largely invented. They grazed his own experience in Italy and Illinois without keeping the central facts in focus. Now he wanted to place his faith in the direct transcription of what he saw. That and no more. Somehow the emotion that he wanted to convey would filter through the reported facts.

From *Ernest Hemingway: A Life Story* by Carlos Baker, New York: Charles Scribner's Sons, 1969, p. 84.

2 **Latin Quarter** the *Quartier Latin* in Paris, a centre for students and artists – 7 **declarative** [dɪ'klærətɪv] making a statement – **scrollwork** ['skrəʊlwɜ:k] decorative design or writing – 10 **to graze** to touch lightly

Hemingway's own most famous statement on the craft of fiction is found in Death in the Afternoon *(1932), a book dealing with bullfighting.*

When writing a novel a writer should create living people; people not characters. A *character* is a caricature. If a writer can make people live there may be no great characters in his book, but it is possible that his book will remain as a whole; as an entity; as a novel. If the people the writer is making talk of old masters; of music; of modern painting; of letters; or of science then they should talk of those subjects in the novel. If they do not talk of those subjects and the writer makes them talk of them he is a faker, and if he talks about them himself to show how much he knows then he is showing off. No matter how good a phrase or a simile he may have if he puts it in where it is not absolutely necessary and irreplaceable he is spoiling his work for egotism. [. . .] A good writer should know as near everything as possible. Naturally he will not. A great enough writer seems to be born with knowledge. But he really is not; he has only been born with the ability to learn in a quicker ratio to the passage of time than other men and without conscious application, and with an intelligence to accept or reject what is already presented as knowledge. [. . .] Every novel which is truly written contributes to the total of knowledge which is there at the disposal of the next writer who comes, but the next writer must pay, always, a certain nominal percentage in experience to be able to understand and assimilate what is available as his birthright and what he must, in turn, take his departure from. If a writer of prose knows enough about what he is writing about he may omit things that he knows and the reader, if the writer is writing truly enough, will have a feeling of those things as strongly as though the writer had stated them. The dignity of movement of an ice-berg is due to only one-eighth of it being above water. A writer who omits things because he does not know them only makes hollow places in his writing.

From *Death in the Afternoon* by Ernest Hemingway, New York: Charles Scribner's Sons, 1950, pp. 191–192.

4 **entity** ['– – –] a self contained being, whole – 5 **letters** *here:* literature – 7 **faker** person who makes s. th. appear genuine, which in fact is not – 9 **simile** ['sɪmɪlɪ] a comparison between essentially unlike things – 14 **ratio** mathematical relationship between two quantities – 15 **application** *here:* effort – 21 **to omit** [əʊ'mɪt] to leave out

Introduction to the Teacher's Book

The Texts

This collection contains five Hemingway stories, each presented in a context of contemporary photographs and supplementary texts. These five parts are prefaced by an introductory section consisting of a biographical note on the first part of Hemingway's career and three excerpts illustrating his ideas on the craft of fiction. The supplementary texts aim to fill in some aspects of the historical, intellectual and biographical background of Hemingway's early work in order to make it more accessible to uninitiated readers half a century later. The inclusion of three poems, one by Hemingway himself, is intended to encourage comparisons of theme, style and genre. In the same way, a sample of Hemingway's journalism is set against a story, and another story is contrasted with and at the same time illustrated by an experimental prose sketch and a dictionary article. It is hoped that this varied presentation will make reading Hemingway more interesting and will encourage students to explore, compare and connect for themselves, and even to look beyond this introductory anthology.

The Ice-Berg Theory

Edgar Allan Poe's 1842 review of Hawthorne's *Twice-Told Tales* stressed that the short tale's characteristic quality should be of having a "unique or single effect" on the reader.[1] Typically, such a unity of impression is achieved by concentrating the narration on a brief moment of crisis, usually of a single character in a single episode. Narratives of this kind are "open at both ends",[2] leaving past conditions and future consequences to be inferred by the reader on the basis of what he has actually been told. Because of the brevity and incompleteness of the action there may be no explicit statement in the story of what the crisis means for the protagonist, and he or the other characters may not be or only partially be aware of its meaning. So it is often left to the reader to spell out the significance of the action. Other

1 Poe's influential review is available in many editions, perhaps most readily in Alfred Weber and Walter F. Greiner, eds., *Short-Story-Theorien (1573–1973)*, Kronberg/Taunus 1977, pp. 34–36.

2 Ian Reid, *The Short Story* (The Critical Idiom 37), London 1977, p. 65.

stories, which depend for their interest mainly on a suprising final twist (like those of O. Henry and Arthur Conan Doyle), make fewer demands on the reader but tend to appear flat on a second reading. By contrast to such "sensation stories" Hemingway's stories in the "scenic method" are memorable and repay discussion (in class or elsewhere) because "the reader is made to work hard in ways comparable to the writer's efforts."[3] As readers, "we are left uncertain about the nature and extent of the revelation, peak of awareness, that a character has apparently experienced. We sense that, while there has been an important shift of perspective in her/his view of things, its significance may not yet have been fully apprehended by that character."[4] This is true of the central figures of all the stories in this collection, with the proviso that it is finally the reader's awareness which makes the most significant progress. In other words, reading a Hemingway story is a matter of active participation. Hemingway had various ways of expressing this relationship between reader and text. Best known is the iceberg metaphor, quoted in the excerpt from *Death in the Afternoon* (**6–7**).

In order to represent an ice-berg it is only necessary to show that part which is visible above water. We all know that seven-eighths of its bulk are hidden below the surface, though we can only guess what it looks like. Similarly, a writer "may omit things that he knows" (**7** 21–22) as long as the part that he depicts is represented accurately and truthfully enough for the reader to be able to reconstruct the hidden parts for himself. The reader, if he really makes the effort, "will have the feeling of those things as strongly as though the writer had stated them" (**7** 22–23). It is for the author to select and omit and to keep "the central fact in focus" (Baker 1969, **6** 11) and for the reader to catch the intended meaning as it "filter[s] through the reported facts" (**6** 13–14).

What is important in teaching Hemingway is to remember that he relies on his readers' ability to contribute their knowledge and experience as complements to each story. This is a further reason why this collection contains supplementary texts; for example, the article on shell-shock (**40**) contains information which can no longer be taken for granted. Other experiences that Hemingway writes about are commonplace enough: fear, courage, pride, humiliation, admiration, disgust, hope, vanity, helpless-

3 Valerie Shaw, *The Short Story: A Critical Introduction,* London 1983, p. 59.

4 Reid 1977, p. 58.

ness, illusion – what Roget classes as "personal affections"[5] and Hemingway simply refers to as "emotions". They are common to all of us who read and yet they are notoriously difficult to understand and talk about. In the writer's focus they become model experiences, no longer private but available for intersubjective attention. This is what Hemingway is getting at when he remarks that "a great enough writer [has] the ability to learn in a quicker ratio to the passage of time than other men" (**6** 12 – **7** 1).

The Simple Style

Hemingway's narrative style is often characterized in a general way as 'simple', 'direct' and 'unambiguous'. His frequent use of repetitive, trivial and even vulgar language has been noted: "Hemingway feels that one short spontaneous vulgarism is more honest than all those grandiloquent slogans which rhetoricians dream up long after the battle. The disparity between rhetoric and experience, which became so evident during the First World War, prompted the twenties to repudiate the genteel stylistic tradition and to accept the American vernacular as our norm of literary discourse."[6] A good example is Hemingway's poem "The Age Demanded" (**13**). This simplicity of style, both in vocabulary and syntax, is the linguistic equivalent of the ice-berg theory. The simple style is basically a strategy for gesturing towards, rather than actually expressing, the baffling and elusive truth of a man's experience. Saying banal things in trivial words may not seem much, but it is the honest thing for Nick Adams or Robert Wilson or Frederic Henry to do. The latter, in *A Farewell to Arms,* makes the point well:

> I did not say anything. I was always embarrassed by the words sacred, glorious, and sacrifice and the expression in vain. We had heard them, sometimes standing in the rain almost out of earshot, so that only the shouted words came through, and had read them, on proclamations that were slapped up by billposters over other proclamations, now for a long time, and I had seen nothing sacred, and the things that were glorious had no glory and the sacrifices were like the stockyards

---

5 Cf. P. M. Roget's *Thesaurus of English Words and Phrases,* first published in 1852 and available in numerous editions. The personal affections are a subgroup of class 6, "Sentient and Moral Powers". This classification is taken up in Wehrle-Eggers, *Deutscher Wortschatz,* Stuttgart 1961, section F "Gefühlsleben". Both works should be available in class.

6 Harry Levin, "Observations on the Style of Ernest Hemingway" (1951), reprinted in: Carlos Baker, ed., *Hemingway and His Critics: An International Anthology,* New York 1961, pp. 93–115, here pp. 102–103.

at Chicago if nothing was done with the meat except to bury it. There were many words that you could not stand to hear and finally only the names of places had dignity. Certain numbers were the same way and certain dates and these with the names of the places were all you could say and have them mean anything. Abstract words such as glory, honour, courage, or hallow were obscene beside the concrete names of villages, the numbers of roads, the names of rivers, the numbers of regiments and the dates. (143–144)

The "simple, declarative sentence" is not, however, one that poses no lexical problems for EFL learners. Hemingway's reliance on unambiguous deictic nouns and his intention of creating a sense of authentic experience led him to employ a considerable amount of technical vocabulary. The language of hunting, fishing and war is so prominent in his stories because it consists of words which designate things, rather than qualities. The devalued abstractions are either parodied (like the parody of the Lord's Prayer in "A Clean, Well-lighted Place"), or reduced to an indeterminate "it" (as in most of the stories in this collection), or replaced by some other equally indeterminate substitute (e.g. the repeated "I feel like hell" of the 3rd soldier in "Today Is Friday").

What does this mean for the teaching of Hemingway? First of all, the student's curiosity to learn "what happens next" in the story should not be impeded by having to look up one difficult word after the other. For a first reading it is sufficient for the student to grasp the theme, the sequence of events and the general argument. Such an approximative reading is also sufficient to get the reader to identify with the actions and emotions of the characters. Many students, used to a different style of working with texts, may even need to be told not to look up every difficult word. In order to support such extensive reading the amount of annotations has been reduced in this edition. It covers only those items necessary to grasp the main aspects of a text. The teacher should also point out that when preparing the texts on the craft of fiction (**5–7**) vocabulary work over and above the annotations is unnecessary. For example: to know exactly where Petoskey lies on the map or what "Wolves and Doughnuts" is about is irrelevant to the objectives pursued with Baker's text. What *is* relevant, and this is what classroom discussions can profitably concentrate on, is the distinction between "ornamental language" and "direct transcription".

The same principle of approximative reading can be brought to bear on the fictional texts. A reader of "The End of Something" is none the wiser if he knows exactly what a "travelling carriage" is. He takes on trust that it is a technical term for some piece of mill equipment, and that is quite enough for the purpose. In the same way, in everyday communication, we identify an "expert" through his use of hard words which we do not understand, and we are impressed by his mastery. The point here is that while Nick can talk fluently on such technical subjects, his emotional problem with Marjorie almost strikes him dumb. Similarly, the Nick of "A Way You'll Never Be" tries to camouflage his real psychological condition by lecturing some Italian soldiers on something quite irrelevant, even if factually true. The language itself is less important than the use to which it is being put, and this use can be recognized by a reader without actually having to understand all of the denotative meaning. A third example: Francis Macomber, after "coming of age" through a successful buffalo hunt, searches awkwardly for suitable words with which to express his new sense of pride and courage. Both his wife and Wilson, though they understand what he is saying, reject his attempt to talk about feelings (**67** 6–14). So there are two distinct lexical spheres in Hemingway's fiction. One world consists of an agreed set of words and expressions to designate factual, impersonal matters. This is safe ground, a matter of learning the vocabulary. By contrast, personal feelings and social relationships, glossed over by everyday conventional phrases, are treacherous ground. To try to put them in words is to hesitate and to falter and to be misunderstood. From the point of view of EFL the first of these spheres can be charted with a dictionary. The second involves acquiring the competence to use unpretentious everyday words in order to communicate the basic emotions which make up a person's identity. In the students' book the technical vocabulary has therefore only been annotated where necessary, additional vocabulary notes being given in this teacher's edition.

Far more attention will need to be paid to how different levels of language (registers) are used in the stories. In a first reading of "Today Is Friday", for example, the word "kike" need only be broadly understood as a swearword, used here in much the same way as "hell" or "Jesus Christ". A second reading will then show how revealingly ambiguous these expressions are, i.e. vocabulary work will lead directly to interpretation. Hemingway's particular use of language, then, becomes a focus of discussion in the second stage of cognitive analysis.

The third stage is that in which the active complementation that we have referred to above takes place.[7] Once the students realize that Nick, Harold Krebs, the Roman soldiers and Francis Macomber are all struggling to find words for what they feel to be true, without ever fully succeeding, and that they can share in this predicament, they will feel encouraged to probe the

---

7 Cf. Heinrich F. Plett, "Text und kommunikative Differenz," *Die neueren Sprachen,* 23 (1974), pp. 31–47, for an account of how indeterminacy leads to complementation.

possibilities and difficulties of "trying to say". Comprehension, analysis and text production are thus three major goals of this course. It is all very well for Nick, in "On Writing", to complain that "talking about everything was bad. Writing about anything actual was bad. It always killed it." One cannot maintain silence about love, fear, admiration, faith and war. Only through learning to talk and learning to write can we hope to come to terms with them.

Nick Adams

Nick Adams is the hero of a number of short stories and sketches. An uncompleted Nick Adams novel was found among Hemingway's papers after his death. All the Nick Adams stories including the ones previously unpublished were collected by Philip Young as *The Nick Adam Stories* in 1972 (available in German, *Die Nick Adams Stories,* rororo 5091). Since students may wish to read other Nick Adams stories than those included in the present collection – and several suggestions to this end are made in the following pages – the chronological sequence of the stories may be helpful:

"Three Shots"
"Indian Camp"
"The Doctor and the Doctor's Wife"
"The Indians Moved Away"

"Ten Indians"
"The End of Something"
"The Three Day Blow"
"The Light of the World"
"The Battler"
"The Killers"
"The Last Good Country"
"Crossing the Mississippi"
"Night Before Landing"

Chapter VI of *In Our Time:* "Nick sat against the wall ..."
"Now I Lay Me"
"A Way You'll Never Be"
"In Another Country"

"Summer People"
"Wedding Day"

"Cross-Country Snow"
"Big Two-Hearted River"
"On Writing"

"An Alpine Idyll"
"A Day's Wait"
"Wine of Wyoming"
"Fathers and Sons"

This is the sequence according to Joseph M. Flora, who explains: "The stories and fragments in the righthand column do not have the authority of the stories in the lefthand column since Hemingway never gave his approval to their publication."[8]

Hemingway chose a telling name for his hero. Adams is first of all a very American name, firmly a part of history and literature. John Adams (1735–1826) was the second President of the U.S.A. from 1797 to 1801, Samuel Adams (1722–1803) was one of the signers of the Declaration of Independence, John Quincy Adams, the son of John, was President from 1825 to 1829. Henry Adams (1838–1918) may round off the list with the autobiographical description of his heritage in *The Education of Henry Adams* (1907 and 1918). Adam is also, of course, the father of man, our common ancestor in his fall from innocence. Conversely, Nick or "Old Nick" commonly refers to the devil, while also being the name of a saint. This complex significance can be traced in the stories. According to Philip Young, "a typical Nick Adams story is of an initiation, is the telling of an event which is violent or evil, or both, or at the very least is the description of an incident which brings the boy into contact with something that is perplexing and unpleasant."[9] The initiation, more briefly, is into the painfulness of life as it really occurs outside the Garden of Eden. The Hemingway hero faces a number of alternatives – whether to face this painfulness, whether to pretend it isn't there, whether to try to hide it or whether to run away from it. One of the most fruitful areas for discussion on any of the stories is to try to find out why one particular decision has been taken, what the alternatives would have meant for the hero, and what exactly it is that he has learnt, in what sense he has grown, like Coleridge's wedding-guest, "a sadder and a wiser man".

The 1925 edition of *In Our Time* contains seven Nick stories, arranged in what is probably the chronological order of Nick's boyhood and young manhood. Nick's exemplary development is naturally of particular interest to students of much about his age – they will feel impelled to compare themselves with the fictional character, to contrast their contemporary situation with the portrait of provincial America (Krebs's Oklahoma, for instance) or of war-torn Europe 70 years ago. It is a composite portrait of a representative American, with Krebs and Macomber contributing. There is

8 Joseph M. Flora, *Hemingway's Nick Adams,* Baton Rouge/London 1982, pp. xiii–xiv.

9 Philip Young, *Ernest Hemingway* (Rinehart Critical Studies), New York 1952, p. 3.

no need to agree with Young and Flora, however, that the stories can only be understood if read as chapters of a whole. Each of the stories makes sense as a self-contained though open-ended unit.

Introductory Lesson

The introductory material on pages 4 to 7 is *not* intended to form the subject of a separate introductory lesson. It can, however, be used to open up certain of the issues which will be at the centre of later lessons.

Assignments

The students can be asked to complete a number of preliminary assignments, using any dictionaries, encylopaedias, etc. at their disposal.
- Complete the biographical note on p. 4.
- Find out which of Hemingway's books are available in German translations, at home, or in the school or public libraries.
- Report on any experience of reading Hemingway or of seeing a film version of any of his stories or novels.
- Discuss what impression of the man you get from the biographical note and from what else you have found out about him.

The Craft of Fiction

The first two texts in this section connect biography and literature, so they form a natural follow-on to the initial assignments. The students can be asked to read both excerpts cursorily, concentrating on the central distinctions.

Stein: What is meant by "seeing things" as opposed to "seeing words" (**5** 22)?
Baker: Explain the double distinction of the "one true simple declarative sentence" versus "scrollwork and ornamental language" and of "central facts in focus" versus "grazing experience" (**6** 5–7, 10–11).

It is quite sufficient for the students to have a general notion of these distinctions at first and to bear them in mind while reading the stories. Their importance will become evident in the course of the reading. This applies particularly to the images of "turning the flame down" (**5** 27) and of the iceberg (**7** 24). The three "Craft of Fiction" texts can therefore serve as rallying points for discussion after reading a story and to give the students a frame of reference for the stories as literary artefacts, as opposed to biography or journalism.

PART I

Ernest Hemingway in the 1930s. Hunting and fishing were to remain a life-long obsession.

The End of Something

In the old days Hortons Bay was a lumbering town. No one who lived in it was out of sound of the big saws in the mill by the lake. Then one year there were no more logs to make lumber. The lumber schooners came into the bay and were loaded with the cut of the mill that stood stacked in the yard. All the piles of lumber were carried away. The big mill building had all its machinery that was removable taken out and hoisted on board one of the schooners by the men who had worked in the mill. The schooner moved out of the bay toward the open lake carrying the two great saws, the travelling carriage that hurled the logs against the revolving, circular saws and all the rollers, wheels, belts and iron piled on a hull-deep load of lumber. Its open hold covered with canvas and lashed tight, the sails of the schooner filled and it moved out into the open lake, carrying with it everything that had made the mill a mill and Hortons Bay a town.

The one-story bunk houses, the eating-house, the company store, the mill offices, and the big mill itself stood deserted in the acres of sawdust that covered the swampy meadow by the shore of the bay.

Ten years later there was nothing of the mill left except the broken white limestone of its foundations showing through the swampy second growth as Nick and Marjorie rowed along the shore. They were trolling along the edge of the channel-bank where the bottom dropped off suddenly from sandy shallows to twelve feet of dark water. They were trolling on their way to the point to set night lines for rainbow trout.

"There's our old ruin, Nick," Marjorie said.

Nick, rowing, looked at the white stone in the green trees.

"There it is," he said.

"Can you remember when it was a mill?" Marjorie asked.

"I can just remember," Nick said.

1 **lumbering town** town dependent on the lumber (wood) industry – 3 **log** tree-trunk that has been cut down – 4 **to stack** to make into a pile – 6 **to hoist** to lift – 9 **to hurl** to throw with great force – 10 **hull** the body of a ship – 11 **hold** part of ship below deck where cargo is stored – **to lash** to fasten with ropes – 14 **bunk house** house where the workers (lumberjacks) sleep in bunks – 15 **deserted** [dɪ'zɜ:tɪd] – 18 **limestone** whitish rock – 19 **to troll** ['trəʊl] to fish with rod and line from a moving boat – 21 **shallows** part of the water which is not deep

"It seems more like a castle," Marjorie said.

Nick said nothing. They rowed on out of sight of the mill, following the shore line. Then Nick cut across the bay.

"They aren't striking," he said.

"No," Marjorie said. She was intent on the rod all the time they trolled, even when she talked. She loved to fish. She loved to fish with Nick.

Close beside the boat a big trout broke the surface of the water. Nick pulled hard on one oar so the boat would turn and the bait spinning far behind would pass where the trout was feeding. As the trout's back came up out of the water the minnows jumped wildly. They sprinkled the surface like a handful of shot thrown into the water. Another trout broke water, feeding on the other side of the boat.

"They're feeding," Marjorie said.

"But they won't strike," Nick said.

He rowed the boat around to troll past both the feeding fish, then headed it for the point. Marjorie did not reel in until the boat touched the shore.

They pulled the boat up the beach and Nick lifted out a pail of live perch. The perch swam in the water in the pail. Nick caught three of them with his hands and cut their heads off and skinned them while Marjorie chased with her hands in the bucket, finally caught a perch, cut its head off and skinned it. Nick looked at her fish.

"You don't want to take the ventral fin out," he said. "It'll be all right for bait but it's better with the ventral fin in."

He hooked each of the skinned perch through the tail. There were two hooks attached to a leader on each rod. Then Marjorie rowed the boat out over the channel-bank, holding the line in her teeth, and looking toward Nick, who stood on the shore holding the rod and letting the line run out from the reel.

"That's about right," he called.

"Should I let it drop?" Marjorie called back, holding the line in her hand.

"Sure. Let it go." Marjorie dropped the line overboard and watched the baits go down through the water.

She came in with the boat and ran the second line out the same way.

4 **to strike** *here:* of fish, to take the bait – 5 **to be intent on** to concentrate one's attention on – 10 **minnow** very small fish (Elritze) – 11 **shot** tiny lead bullets fired from a shotgun – 16 **to reel in** to pull in the line – 17 **pail** bucket – **perch** edible freshwater fish (Flußbarsch) – 22 **you don't want to** *here:* there's no need to, you shouldn't – **ventral fin** (Bauchflosse) – 25 **leader** transparent line used for fishing

Each time Nick set a heavy slab of driftwood across the butt of the rod to hold it solid and propped it up at an angle with a small slab. He reeled in the slack line so the line ran taut out to where the bait rested on the sandy floor of the channel and set the click on the reel. When a trout, feeding on the bottom, took the bait it would run with it, taking line out of the reel in a rush and making the reel sing with the click on.

Marjorie rowed up the point a little way so she would not disturb the line. She pulled hard on the oars and the boat went way up the beach. Little waves came in with it. Marjorie stepped out of the boat and Nick pulled the boat high up the beach.

"What's the matter, Nick?" Marjorie asked.

"I don't know," Nick said, getting wood for a fire.

They made a fire with driftwood. Marjorie went to the boat and brought a blanket. The evening breeze blew the smoke toward the point, so Marjorie spread the blanket out between the fire and the lake.

Marjorie sat on the blanket with her back to the fire and waited for Nick. He came over and sat down beside her on the blanket. In back of them was the close second-growth timber of the point and in front was the bay with the mouth of Hortons Creek. It was not quite dark. The fire-light went as far as the water. They could both see the two steel rods at an angle over the dark water. The fire glinted on the reels.

Marjorie unpacked the basket of supper.

"I don't feel like eating," said Nick.

"Come on and eat, Nick."

"All right."

They ate without talking, and watched the two rods and the fire-light in the water.

"There's going to be a moon tonight," said Nick. He looked across the bay to the hills that were beginning to sharpen against the sky. Beyond the hills he knew the moon was coming up.

"I know it," Marjorie said happily.

"You know everything," Nick said.

"Oh, Nick, please cut it out! Please, please don't be that way!"

"I can't help it," Nick said. "You do. You know everything. That's the trouble. You know you do."

1 **slab** thick flat piece of s. th. – **driftwood** wood washed up on the beach – **butt** thick end – 2 **to prop s. th. up** to support – 3 **slack** loose – **taut** [tɔ:t] opposite of slack – 4 **click** gadget fitted on a reel which makes a clicking noise when a fish pulls on the line (Bißanzeige) – 21 **to glint** to reflect light, *here:* to be reflected

Marjorie did not say anything.

"I've taught you everything. You know you do. What don't you know, anyway?"

"Oh, shut up," Marjorie said. "There comes the moon."

They sat on the blanket without touching each other and watched the moon rise.

"You don't have to talk silly," Marjorie said. "What's really the matter?"

"I don't know."

"Of course you know."

"No I don't."

"Go on and say it."

Nick looked on at the moon, coming up over the hills.

"It isn't fun any more."

He was afraid to look at Marjorie. Then he looked at her. She sat there with her back toward him. He looked at her back. "It isn't fun any more. Not any of it."

She didn't say anything. He went on. "I feel as though everything was gone to hell inside of me. I don't know, Marge. I don't know what to say."

He looked on at her back.

"Isn't love any fun?" Marjorie said.

"No," Nick said. Marjorie stood up. Nick sat there, his head in his hands.

"I'm going to take the boat," Marjorie called to him. "You can walk back around the point."

"All right," Nick said. "I'll push the boat off for you."

"You don't need to," she said. She was afloat in the boat on the water with the moonlight on it. Nick went back and lay down with his face in the blanket by the fire. He could hear Marjorie rowing on the water.

He lay there for a long time. He lay there while he heard Bill come into the clearing walking around through the woods. He felt Bill coming up to the fire. Bill didn't touch him, either.

"Did she go all right?" Bill said.

"Yes," Nick said, lying, his face on the blanket.

"Have a scene?"

"No, there wasn't any scene."

"How do you feel?"

"Oh, go away, Bill! Go away for a while."

Bill selected a sandwich from the lunch basket and walked over to have a look at the rods.

Interpretation and Teaching Notes

Background

This story is taken from Hemingway's first collection, *In Our Time,* published in October 1925. As the two texts, pp. 5 and 6, by Gertrude Stein and Carlos Baker show, Hemingway, in his early twenties, was gradually moving towards his own distinctive style of story telling. He had been writing short fiction ever since his high school days, increasingly on subjects related to his personal experiences of hunting, fishing, sex and war. "The End of Something", linking two of these areas of experience, is autobiographical to the extent that the village of Horton Bay (spelt without an -s) on Lake Charlevoix was where the Hemingways went for weekend fishing trips and where his childhood friend Wesley Dilworth came from. The name Marjorie is remembered from Marjorie Bump, a girl Hemingway got to know at the Dilworth's small restaurant overlooking the lake. It was in the Methodist Church at Horton Bay that Hemingway and Hadley Richardson were married on September 3rd, 1921. This biographical background in no way explains Hemingway's fiction – it is just the material which he reworked imaginatively till its significance went far beyond the original occasion.

In Our Time

The title of the collection *In Our Time* is relevant. On the cover of the 1924 collection of vignettes titled *in our time* (incorporated as the interchapters in the 1925 edition) was a montage of newspaper headlines, an allusion to its author's work as a journalist and also to the contemporary nature of the texts within.[1] Philip Young, noting Hemingway's habit of random quotation, takes the title to be "a sardonic allusion to that phrase from the *Book of Common Prayer* which Neville Chamberlain was later to make notorious".[2] Chamberlain did not use the phrase "peace for our time" till 1938 when he commented on the Munich Agreement on the Sudetenland crisis, so Hemingway cannot have intended to allude to Chamberlain's and

1 There is a facsimile of this cover in Georges-Albert Astre, *Ernest Hemingway in Selbstzeugnissen und Dokumenten,* Hamburg 1961 (rororo bildmonographien 73), p. 51.
2 Young 1952, p. 2.

Daladier's policy of appeasement towards Hitler. Nevertheless, the *Book of Common Prayer's* "Give peace in our time, O Lord" may well have seemed provokingly optimistic to a writer who had witnessed the atrocities of World War I in Italy and of the Graeco-Turkish War of 1922. The title may also be seen as an invitation to dialogue between writer and reader, "our time" being the common experience of both.

Structure

At a first glance, "The End of Something" is a simple enough story. There are only three characters – Nick and Marjorie, and then right at the end their mutual friend Bill. The setting is briefly and accurately described as the derelict lumbering town of Hortons Bay on the shore of "the lake", i. e. Lake Charlevoix. Nick and Marjorie are spending a couple of days fishing on the lake. Several hints in the text show that they have often been there together and that they share memories and experiences connected with earlier outings. There is only one direct indication of time in the story ("Ten years later ..." **9** 17). This, together with what we know of the biographical background, suggests that Nick and Marjorie are about sixteen or seventeen.

Structurally the story consists of two balanced halves, each of which can be seen to divide into two further parts. As the following chart shows, a general discussion of how the story is put together can be started by putting any of a number of questions:

- What are the events that are narrated in the story?
- Is the story about past, present or future events?
- Which parts of the story did you find difficult to read and which were easy?

The answers to such questions will help the students to correlate "story" and "theme", especially when notes are taken, e. g. on the blackboard. The history of Hortons Bay, its passage from prosperity to decay parallels and comments on the gradual decline in the relationship between Nick and Marjorie. Both are in turn paralleled by the setting of the sun and the rise of the moon. In the telling of the story no explicit linking of these elements is given – the unobtrusive narrator simply provides the "facts". The story can therefore be approached by collecting these facts and gradually linking them up with each other. The teacher should not keep too tight a hand on the students' ideas on what is significant and what is not, so the chart can be expanded by adding further columns to accommodate students' remarks on symbols, etc.

The Structure

section	page/line	time	time of day	events	narrative mode	language	etc.
I	**9** 1–16	past: "in the old days"	---	dismantling the lumbering town	summary, description	technical vocabulary	
II	**9** 17 – **11** 11	present: "ten years later"	evening (**11** 14)	M. and N. fishing	report and dialogue	simple dialogue, complex report	
III	**11** 12 – **12** 27	present	later evening	M. and N. talking at the fire	mostly dialogue, some report	simple	
IV	**12** 28–38	present (to future?)	night	M. rows away, Nick at the fire, Bill arrives	dialogue and report	simple	

First Unit: Action, Scene and Symbol

Most readers' first impression of this story is that it is in all respects very unspectacular. There is no fast-moving action, no surprising turn of events, no ironic reversal or neat solution. If these traditional elements of the short story are absent, there is nevertheless an element of tradition in the story's title, which takes up the tradition of riddle telling: the end of what? This is what interests us in the gradual unfolding of the relationship between Nick and Marjorie – what has gone wrong and why?

In assigning the story to be read before the first lesson the teacher can ask the students to work out (in brief, written notes) their provisional answers to these questions.

Various answers have been proposed: the end of a young man's illusions about romantic love[3], the recognition that falling out of love happens as easily as falling in love[4]. According to a third reading, "the something in the story's title is not Nick's feeling for Marjorie; rather it is their relationship. The story marks the end of something that means a good deal to Nick, something that he is not even sure he wants to end."[5]

1. *The ruined saw-mill where the action takes place is described in detail (**9** 1–16) but is not mentioned again in the course of the story. Why is it described at all? Could the story have begun a page later?*

a) The description of Hortons Bay provides an authentic backdrop. The specific detail in this first section contrasts with the lack of detail about Nick and Marjorie in the later sections.

b) Hortons Bay constitutes an important part of Nick's and Marjorie's identity. They can both remember when the mill still flourished (**9** 26–27). The ruins seem to have been the setting for earlier stages of their love affair (**9** 23, note the possessive pronoun).

c) The description is not just of town and mill, but of their decline. The mill is no longer a mill, the town no longer a town (**9** 13). In this sense the decline of Hortons Bay prefigures the development of Nick's relationship to Marjorie.

---

3 Robert W. Lewis, *Hemingway on Love,* Austin/London 1965, p. 9.

4 Clinton S. Burhans, "The Complex Unity of *In Our Time,*" in Jackson J. Benson, ed., *The Short Stories of Ernest Hemingway: Critical Essays,* Durham 1975, p. 22, quoted by Flora 1982.

5 Flora 1982, p. 57.

d) – Yes, the story could have started at **9** 19, leaving out **9** 23 to **10** 3. The first part doesn't tell us anything about Nick and Marjorie.
– No, the story wouldn't make sense without the introduction.
For example, when Nick doesn't respond to Marjorie's imaginative interpretation of the mill ruins as a castle (**10** 1–2) you can tell that they don't fit together, that they don't share the same ideas.

The next set of questions focuses on Hemingway's economy of narration, the choice of a central action which omits both the past and subsequent action.

2. *What is the reader told about Nick's and Marjorie's past? Is there anything else you would like to know about Nick and Marjorie?*
a) Nick and Marjorie, who must be about 16 or 17 years old, have known Hortons Bay ten years earlier (**9** 17) and have been there together often since. Nick seems to have taught Marjorie quite a lot about fishing – she still appears as the pupil, he as the teacher (**10** 22–23, 29–31). This is made explicit later on (**11** 31 – **12** 3).
b) We are not told what Nick and Marjorie look like, there are no details of how they got to know each other, whether they have quarrelled seriously before, etc.

The students should be encouraged to point out the "missing biography". Hemingway does not indiscriminately heap detail on detail but selects those items of information, those suggestive hints which induce the reader to infer facts, events and motives. The teacher can use this opportunity to introduce the concept of the reticent or non-intrusive narrator. In Wayne C. Booth's terminology the narrator of "The End of Something" is "impersonal", i.e. there is no sense of the narrator of the story having a separate identity.[6] For the reader this means that there is no narrator who intrudes and helps along with evaluative comment and summary (cf. the column "Narrative Mode" in the chart p. 25).

Talking about the meaning of the ruined mill will almost inevitably prompt the students to introduce the concept of symbol. A literary symbol is the use of an image to suggest and make intelligible an idea. There is usually no visual resemblance between the image and the intended idea. Both a literal and a figurative interpretation are possible.[7]

---

6 Wayne C. Booth, *The Rhetoric of Fiction,* Chicago 1961, especially the section on undramatized narrators, pp. 151–152.

7 Cf. the *Princeton Encyclopedia of Poetry and Poetics,* ed. Alex Preminger, New York/London ^{2}1974, s. v. "Symbol".

Second Unit: Knowing and Saying

One of Hemingway's narrative techniques is repetition. "We need make no word count to be sure that his literary vocabulary, with foreign and technical exceptions, consists of relatively few and short words. The corollary, of course, is that every word sees a good deal of hard use."[8]

From **11** 11 on, i.e. with the beginning of section III of the story, the repetition of "know" is very noticeable.

1. *Find examples of things that Nick is good at doing or "knows". What are the things he does not know, or know about?*
Similar questions may be asked about Marjorie. The students' answers can be sorted out on the blackboard or taken down in note form as the result of group work.

Nick knows/can do		**Nick doesn't know/know about**	
		10 2	imagining a castle
10 4	when fish strike (also **10** 14)		
10 22	how to prepare bait		
10 31	when to drop the line		
11 2	how to prop a rod		
		11 12	what's wrong
11 28	when there'll be a moon		
		11 32	accepting Marjorie's competence about things like her knowledge about the moon rising
		12 8, 10	what's the matter
		12 18	what to say

The students can be asked to summarize each of the columns: Nick knows all about fishing and life in the open, but he can't share Marjorie's thoughts, nor accept that she is almost as good at fishing as he is. He can't put his feelings in words.

Such a summary can then be compared with the class's findings on Marjorie. The above chart shows quite clearly what kind of development Nick goes through in the course of the story. It is a gradually unveiled loss of competence contrasted with Marjorie's growing self-confidence and even independence.

8 Levin 1951, p. 105.

The linguistically most interesting aspect of Nick's problem, and therefore the one most relevant to language teaching, is the conflict of knowing and saying. In a field like fishing, language is easy to use because words refer unambiguously to things and to how to do things. A perch is a perch, a reel is a reel. By contrast, the language for acting out and analysing personal relations and feelings is not at Nick's disposal. He has not learned this kind of language, nor has he learned to want to talk about such subjects. Further, as long as he can give Marjorie instructions and correct her, Nick is using language to dominate. Nick's domination is undermined as Marjorie becomes more and more capable, it wholly collapses as the fishing is over and they move on to subjects he is not confident about. This seems to be the root of their problem.

2. *What, in Nick's view, is wrong with Marjorie "knowing everything"? Do you think he is right to be upset?*
a) Nick can't stand Marjorie being his equal. She's almost as good at fishing as he is, she can row well, she knows about the rhythm of the moon. She is almost independent of him. Also, he doesn't like being pushed into giving explanations of how he feels. Most people don't like that.
b) – People often avoid expressing their thoughts and feelings. In our TV-dominated culture it is becoming difficult to talk to other people, e.g. one's parents.
– It is always difficult to talk about personal matters like friendship, love, envy, etc. People often become aggressive when pressure is put on them to express their feelings (**11** 32–35, **12** 2–7). Men are or used to be brought up *not* to express their feelings. I'm not surprised Nick is upset. He feels weak because he doesn't know how to get on with Marjorie and because he can't say what he feels.

The photograph on p. 8 can be discussed at this point. In what role is Hemingway posing here? What image of himself is he trying to project? See also the photograph on p. 41.

Third Unit: Plot and Ending

The purpose of this unit is to exploit the open-ended nature of the story. This basic characteristic of the genre, together wirth the knowing-saying conflict discussed above, permits the students to become linguistically active in Nick's stead, using their own experience. The inconclusive ending of the story also provides the impetus for follow-up reading of further Nick Adams stories. It is suggested that the students write down their "answers" to the following questions in as full a form as possible (not just as notes or summaries) and that these be pooled in group work and/or discussed individually.

1. *Try to say for Nick what he can't say for himself (cf.* ***12*** *18).*
I think what Nick is trying to say, what he feels deep down, is that Marjorie doesn't seem to need him any more. He's taught her everything he knows about fishing, rowing, making a driftwood fire, all about outdoor life. Their relationship no longer works the way it used to, with him dominating her, and her accepting his dominance. They have got to a point where their relationship will either change into something new or really come to an end. Nick seems to have rather a limited, conventional view of what a boy – girl relationship should be. The word "love", introduced by Marjorie, is only a very unspecific label. It means something different to each of them. Or it is just a conventional word and Nick doesn't know whether it really describes his own experience.

Homework: Write a letter, either from Nick's or from Marjorie's point of view, explaining "what is really the matter".

2. *Why doesn't Nick give a proper answer when Bill asks him how he feels (**12** 35)? How do you think he does feel?*
a) Nick is too busy trying to come to terms with himself to give Bill an answer. He is experiencing a new feeling, one for which he (as yet) has no words. He realizes that his behaviour was basically immature and that Marjorie has proved her superiority to him.
b) The question "How do you think he feels?" can best be answered in a brain storming session. For this, each student writes a word or short phrase on a slip of paper, e.g. "angry", "sad", "disappointed", etc. The teacher collects the slips and sticks them on the blackboard as they come and without commenting. When no more answers are forthcoming (after about ten minutes) the slips can be sorted out and discussed, and new ideas can be incorporated.

3. *Do you think that Nick's affair with Marjorie has really come to an end? How will their story/stories continue? Discuss in class and then read "The Three Day Blow".*
As regards action, one episode in Nick's life has come to an end. Is it, however, true to say that Nick has reached an end in the sense of having attained a new state of awareness, or that his character has changed in any

way, or that the finds himself in a completely new situation? These are the kinds of changes that usually constitute the unity of a plot.[9] In a short story like this there is no completed change – the same could be said of all the other stories in this reader.

A number of alternatives are possible for a continuation of the story:
a) reconciliation: Nick and Marjorie can have a heart-to-heart talk and attempt to re-define their respective roles (cf. the "second growth" in Hortons Bay, **9** 18);
b) open quarrel: a chance meeting a couple of days later might lead to an open quarrel leading either to reconciliation or final estrangement;
c) passive separation: Nick and Marjorie drift apart, avoid each other, take no active measures to continue their relationship, choose new friends, engage in ersatz activities (in Nick's case things like getting drunk, hunting, etc.).

For Further Study

Read "The Three Day Blow." Other stories, e.g. "Cross-Country Snow," can also be read as continuations.

Additional Vocabulary

A number of vocabulary items are visualized in the photograph on p. **8** (rod, reel, ventral fin, dorsal fin).

9 8–9 **travelling carriage** (Sägeschlitten)

10 10 **to sprinkle** to throw a light shower of something on a surface, *here:* to break the surface of the water as if something had been sprinkled on it

11 18 **second-growth timber** small trees and bushes that grow where big trees have been cut down

---

9 Cf. Norman Friedman, "Forms of the Plot" (1955), repr. in Philip Stevick, ed., *The Theory of the Novel,* London/New York 1967, pp. 145–166. Friedman proposes that a plot can be analysed by applying three questions to it: 1) "Who is the protagonist?", 2) "what is his or her character, and how do we respond to it? What is his or her fortune, and do we fear it will become worse and hope it will become better? And what is his or her thought, and do we feel he or she is sufficiently aware of the facts of the situation and the consequences of his or her behavior in order to be held responsible for what he or she does and undergoes?" and 3) "which of these three factors undergoes a change as the plot unfolds and reaches its conclusions?" (pp. 154–155).

PART II

Back home in Oak Park, April 1919.

The Age Demanded

The age demanded that we sing
And cut away our tongue.

The age demanded that we flow
And hammered in the bung.

The age demanded that we dance
And jammed us into iron pants.

And in the end the age was handed
The sort of shit that it demanded.

Originally published in *Der Querschnitt*, February, 1925. Reprinted from *The Collected Poems of Ernest Hemingway*, Folcroft, Pa.: Folcroft Library, 1973.

bung stopper (of cork, etc.) for closing a barrel
to jam into to squeeze into

14

Soldier's Home

Krebs went to the war from a Methodist college in Kansas. There is a picture which shows him among his fraternity brothers, all of them wearing exactly the same height and style collar. He enlisted in the Marines in 1917 and did not return to the United States until the second division returned from the Rhine in the summer of 1919.

There is a picture which shows him on the Rhine with two German girls and another corporal. Krebs and the corporal look too big for their uniforms. The German girls are not beautiful. The Rhine does not show in the picture.

By the time Krebs returned to his home town in Oklahoma the greeting of heroes was over. He came back much too late. The men from the town who had been drafted had all been welcomed elaborately on their return. There had been a great deal of hysteria. Now the reaction had set in. People seemed to think it was rather ridiculous for Krebs to be getting back so late, years after the war was over.

At first Krebs, who had been at Belleau Wood, Soissons, the Champagne, St. Mihiel and in the Argonne did not want to talk about the war at all. Later he felt the need to talk but no one wanted to hear about it. His town had heard too many atrocity stories to be thrilled by actualities. Krebs found that to be listened to at all he had to lie, and after he had done this twice he, too, had a reaction against the war and against talking about it. A distaste for everything that had happened to him in the war set in because of the lies he had told. All of the times that had been able to make him feel cool and clear inside himself when he thought of them; the times so long back when he had done the one thing, the only thing for a man to do, easily and naturally, when he might have done something else, now lost their cool, valuable quality and then were lost themselves.

His lies were quite unimportant lies and consisted in attributing to himself

2 **fraternity** [frəˈtɜ:nɪtɪ] *AE* student society – 3 **to enlist** to join the armed forces – **the Marines** a branch of the U.S. Navy trained for land and sea operations – 12 **to draft** to call up for military service – **elaborately** [ɪˈlæbərətlɪ] with a lot of ceremony – 13 **hysteria** [hɪsˈtɪərɪə] –19 **atrocity** [əˈtrɒsɪtɪ] cruel acts – **actualities** *here:* things that had actually happened – 28 **to attribute to** [əˈtrɪbju:t] to credit

things other men had seen, done or heard of, and stating as facts certain apocryphal incidents familiar to all soldiers. Even his lies were not sensational at the pool room. His acquaintances, who had heard detailed accounts of German women found chained to machine guns in the Argonne forest and who could not comprehend, or were barred by their patriotism from interest in, any German machine gunners who were not chained, were not thrilled by his stories.

Krebs acquired the nausea in regard to experience that is the result of untruth or exaggeration, and when he occasionally met another man who had really been a soldier and they talked a few minutes in the dressing room at a dance he fell into the easy pose of the old soldier among other soldiers: that he had been badly, sickeningly frightened all the time. In this way he lost everything.

During this time, it was late summer, he was sleeping late in bed, getting up to walk down town to the library to get a book, eating lunch at home, reading on the front porch until he became bored and then walking down through the town to spend the hottest hours of the day in the cool dark of the pool room. He loved to play pool.

In the evening he practised on his clarinet, strolled down town, read and went to bed. He was still a hero to his two young sisters. His mother would have given him breakfast in bed if he had wanted it. She often came in when he was in bed and asked him to tell her about the war, but her attention always wandered. His father was non-committal.

Before Krebs went away to the war he had never been allowed to drive the family motor car. His father was in the real estate business and always wanted the car to be at his command when he required it to take clients out into the country to show them a piece of farm property. The car always stood outside the First National Bank building where his father had an office on the second floor. Now, after the war, it was still the same car.

Nothing was changed in the town except that the young girls had grown up. But they lived in such a complicated world of already defined alliances and shifting feuds that Krebs did not feel the energy or the courage to break into it. He liked to look at them, though. There were so many good-looking

2 **apocryphal** [əˈpɒkrɪfl] of doubtful truth, fictitious – 3 **pool room** *AE* room where pool-billiard is played – 5 **to bar** to prevent – 8 **nausea** [ˈnɔ:zjə] feeling of sickness – 16 **porch** covered doorway, veranda – 23 **non-committal** not showing what one thinks – 25 **real estate** immovable property such as land and houses – 32 **to shift** to change – **feud** [fju:d] quarrel

young girls. Most of them had their hair cut short. When he went away only little girls wore their hair like that or girls that were fast. They all wore sweaters and shirt waists with round Dutch collars. It was a pattern. He liked to look at them from the front porch as they walked on the other side of the street. He liked to watch them walking under the shade of the trees. He liked the round Dutch collars above their sweaters. He liked their silk stockings and flat shoes. He liked their bobbed hair and the way they walked.

When he was in town their appeal to him was not very strong. He did not like them when he saw them in the Greek's ice cream parlor. He did not want them themselves really. They were too complicated. There was something else. Vaguely he wanted a girl but he did not want to have to work to get her. He would have liked to have a girl but he did not want to have to spend a long time getting her. He did not want to get into the intrigue and the politics. He did not want to have to do any courting. He did not want to tell any more lies. It wasn't worth it.

He did not want any consequences. He did not want any consequences ever again. He wanted to live along without consequences. Besides he did not really need a girl. The army had taught him that. It was all right to pose as though you had to have a girl. Nearly everybody did that. But it wasn't true. You did not need a girl. That was the funny thing. First a fellow boasted how girls mean nothing to him, that he never thought of them, that they could not touch him. Then a fellow boasted that he could not get along without girls, that he had to have them all the time, that he could not go to sleep without them.

That was all a lie. It was all a lie both ways. You did not need a girl unless you thought about them. He learned that in the army. Then sooner or later you always got one. When you were really ripe for a girl you always got one. You did not have to think about it. Sooner or later it would come. He had learned that in the army.

Now he would have liked a girl if she had come to him and not wanted to talk. But here at home it was all too complicated. He knew he could never get through it all again. It was not worth the trouble. That was the thing about French girls and German girls. There was not all this talking. You couldn't talk much and you did not need to talk. It was simple and you were

2 **fast** *dated slang* addicted to pleasure, immoral – 3 **shirt waist** *AE* woman's plain blouse – 7 **bobbed hair** hair cut shorter than shoulder length – 15 **to court a girl** to try to win a girl's affections – 21 **to boast** to praise o. s. in an exaggerated way

friends. He thought about France and then he began to think about Germany. On the whole he had liked Germany better. He did not want to leave Germany. He did not want to come home. Still, he had come home. He sat on the front porch.

He liked the girls that were walking along the other side of the street. He liked the look of them much better than the French girls or the German girls. But the world they were in was not the world he was in. He would like to have one of them. But it was not worth it. They were such a nice pattern. He liked the pattern. It was exciting. But he would not go through all the talking. He did not want one badly enough. He liked to look at them all, though. It was not worth it. Not now when things were getting good again.

He sat there on the porch reading a book on the war. It was a history and he was reading about all the engagements he had been in. It was the most interesting reading he had ever done. He wished there were more maps. He looked forward with a good feeling to reading all the really good histories when they would come out with good detail maps. Now he was really learning about the war. He had been a good soldier. That made a difference.

One morning after he had been home about a month his mother came into his bedroom and sat on the bed. She smoothed her apron.

"I had a talk with your father last night, Harold," she said, "and he is willing for you to take the car out in the evenings."

"Yeah?" said Krebs, who was not fully awake. "Take the car out? Yeah?"

"Yes. Your father has felt for some time that you should be able to take the car out in the evenings whenever you wished but we only talked it over last night."

"I'll bet you made him," Krebs said.

"No. It was your father's suggestion that we talk the matter over."

"Yeah. I'll bet you made him," Krebs sat up in bed.

"Will you come down to breakfast, Harold?" his mother said.

"As soon as I get my clothes on," Krebs said.

His mother went out of the room and he could hear her frying something downstairs while he washed, shaved and dressed to go down into the dining-room for breakfast. While he was eating breakfast his sister brought in the mail.

"Well, Hare," she said. "You old sleepy-head. What do you ever get up for?"

Krebs looked at her. He liked her. She was his best sister.

13 **engagement** *here:* battle – 19 **to smooth** [smu:ð] to wipe away the folds with one's hand

"Have you got the paper?" he asked.

She handed him *The Kansas City Star* and he shucked off its brown wrapper and opened it to the sporting page. He folded *The Star* open and propped it against the water pitcher with his cereal dish to steady it, so he could read while he ate.

"Harold," his mother stood in the kitchen doorway, "Harold, please don't muss up the paper. Your father can't read his *Star* if it's been mussed."

"I won't muss it," Krebs said.

His sister sat down at the table and watched him while he read.

"We're playing indoor over at school this afternoon," she said. "I'm going to pitch."

"Good," said Krebs. "How's the old wing?"

"I can pitch better than lots of the boys. I tell them all you taught me. The other girls aren't much good."

"Yeah?" said Krebs.

"I tell them all you're my beau. Aren't you my beau, Hare?"

"You bet."

"Couldn't your brother really be your beau just because he's your brother?"

"I don't know."

"Sure you know. Couldn't you be my beau, Hare, if I was old enough and if you wanted to?"

"Sure. You're my girl now."

"Am I really your girl?"

"Sure."

"Do you love me?"

"Uh, huh."

"Will you love me always?"

"Sure."

"Will you come over and watch me play indoor?"

"Maybe."

"Aw, Hare, you don't love me. If you loved me, you'd want to come over and watch me play indoor."

Krebs's mother came into the dining-room from the kitchen. She carried a plate with two fried eggs and some crisp bacon on it and a plate of buckwheat cakes.

2 **to shuck off** *AE* to remove – 4 **pitcher** a large jug – 7 **to muss up** to put into disorder – 10 **indoor** *here:* indoor baseball – 11 **to pitch** to throw the ball, as in baseball – 12 **wing** *slang* baseball player's pitching arm – 16 **beau** [bəʊ] boyfriend

"You run along, Helen," she said. "I want to talk to Harold."

She put the eggs and bacon down in front of him and brought in a jug of maple syrup for the buckwheat cakes. Then she sat down across the table from Krebs.

"I wish you'd put down the paper a minute, Harold," she said.

Krebs took down the paper and folded it.

"Have you decided what you are going to do yet, Harold?" his mother said, taking off her glasses.

"No," said Krebs.

"Don't you think it's about time?" His mother did not say this in a mean way. She seemed worried.

"I hadn't thought about it," Krebs said.

"God has some work for everyone to do," his mother said. "There can be no idle hands in His Kingdom."

"I'm not in His Kingdom," Krebs said.

"We are all of us in His Kingdom."

Krebs felt embarrassed and resentful as always.

"I've worried about you so much, Harold," his mother went on. "I know the temptations you must have been exposed to. I know how weak men are. I know what your own dear grandfather, my own father, told us about the Civil War and I have prayed for you. I pray for you all day long, Harold."

Krebs looked at the bacon fat hardening on his plate.

"Your father is worried, too," his mother went on. "He thinks you have lost your ambition, that you haven't got a definite aim in life. Charley Simmons, who is just your age, has a good job and is going to be married. The boys are all settling down; they're all determined to get somewhere; you can see that boys like Charley Simmons are on their way to being really a credit to the community."

Krebs said nothing.

"Don't look that way, Harold," his mother said. "You know we love you and I want to tell you for your own good how matters stand. Your father does not want to hamper your freedom. He thinks you should be allowed to drive the car. If you want to take some of the nice girls out riding with you, we are only too pleased. We want you to enjoy yourself. But you are going to have to settle down to work, Harold. Your father doesn't care what you start in at. All work is honorable as he says. But you've got to make a start

3 **maple syrup** (Ahornsirup) – 17 **resentful** [rɪˈzentfəl] bitter – 27 **a credit to s. th.** a source of honour for s. th., s. th. or s. o. to be proud of – 32 **to hamper** to get in the way of – 33 **riding** *here:* for a drive

at something. He asked me to speak to you this morning and then you can stop in and see him at his office."

"Is that all?" Krebs said.

"Yes. Don't you love your mother, dear boy?"

"No," Krebs said.

His mother looked at him across the table. Her eyes were shiny. She started crying.

"I don't love anybody," Krebs said.

It wasn't any good. He couldn't tell her, he couldn't make her see it. It was silly to have said it. He had only hurt her. He went over and took hold of her arm. She was crying with her head in her hands.

"I didn't mean it," he said. "I was just angry at something. I didn't mean I didn't love you."

His mother went on crying. Krebs put his arm on her shoulder.

"Can't you believe me, mother?"

His mother shook her head.

"Please, please, mother. Please believe me."

"All right," his mother said chokily. She looked up at him. "I believe you, Harold."

Krebs kissed her hair. She put her face up to him.

"I'm your mother," she said. "I held you next to my heart when you were a tiny baby."

Krebs felt sick and vaguely nauseated.

"I know, Mummy," he said. "I'll try and be a good boy for you."

"Would you kneel and pray with me, Harold?" his mother asked.

They knelt down beside the dining-room table and Krebs's mother prayed.

"Now, you pray, Harold," she said.

"I can't," Krebs said.

"Try, Harold."

"I can't."

"Do you want me to pray for you?"

"Yes."

So his mother prayed for him and then they stood up and Krebs kissed his mother and went out of the house. He had tried so to keep his life from being complicated. Still, none of it had touched him. He had felt sorry for his mother and she had made him lie. He would go to Kansas City and get a

18 **choky** prevented from breathing freely

job and she would feel all right about it. There would be one more scene maybe before he got away. He would not go down to his father's office. He would miss that one. He wanted his life to go smoothly. It had just gotten going that way. Well, that was all over now, anyway. He would go over to the schoolyard and watch Helen play indoor baseball.

Bombardment

Four days the earth was rent and torn
By bursting steel,
The houses fell about us;
Three nights we dared not sleep,
Sweating, and listening for the imminent crash
Which meant our death.

The fourth night every man,
Nerve-tortured, racked to exhaustion,
Slept, muttering and twitching,
While the shells crashed overhead.

The fifth day there came a hush;
We left our holes
And looked above the wreckage of the earth
To where the white clouds moved in silent lines
Across the untroubled blue.

By Richard Aldington (1892–1962). The poem originally appeared in *Images of War. A Book of Poems,* Westminster: The Beaumont Press, 1919.

1 **rent** past participle of *to rend:* torn (*literary*) – 5 **imminent** which will happen very soon – 8 **to rack** to torture, as on the *rack*, an instrument of torture – 9 **to twitch** to move in an uncontrolled manner, to tremble – 11 **hush** silence, stillness

Interpretation and Teaching Notes

Background

The autobiographical background to "Soldier's Home" is the end of what Baker calls "the most romantic chapter in the first twenty years of his life".[1] Hemingway returned to the U.S.A. from Italy on January 21st, 1919, proud of his war experiences and marked for life not only by the 227 scars on his legs caused by a mortar bomb at Fossalta. He seems very soon to have felt homesick for Italy and especially for Agnes von Kurowsky, the American nurse he had fallen in love with. He struck his sister Marcelline as lonely, but no one else in the family seemed to notice. The photograph on p. 13 (see also p. 28) shows Hemingway in his Italian officer's uniform at home in Oak Park, where homecoming parties were held in his honour. He gave several talks on the war, making a great impression by reporting on "the mortar explosion that had scared him so badly in July. He told of carrying the wounded soldier back to the command post, and held up for inspection his incredibly torn and blood-stained uniform breeches. ... He told of having met an Arditi captain who plugged the bullet holes in his chest with cigarette stubs and went on fighting."[2] Showing off, telling tall tales, being feted as a hero were all a part of the difficult process of settling down to post-war civilian life. As with Krebs, "a distaste for everything that had happened to him in the war set in" (**14** 21–22), especially when in March 1919 Agnes, whom he had been writing to daily, wrote to tell him that she had fallen in love with a young Italian officer. He felt hurt and angry, but got over it by going on fishing trips and having drinking parties with his friends. His parents did not appreciate the parties and after an incident in 1920[3] his mother Grace, refusing to talk with him, wrote him the following letter:

> Unless you, my son Ernest, come to yourself; cease your lazy loafing and pleasure seeking; borrowing with no thought of returning; stop trying to graft a living off anybody and everybody; spending all your earnings lavishly and wastefully on luxuries for yourself; stop trading on your handsome face to fool little gullible girls, and neglecting your duties to God and your Savior, Jesus Christ; unless, in other words, you come into your manhood, there is nothing before you but

---

1 Baker 1969, p. 93. Book 2, Chapter 7 of Baker's biography is entitled "Soldier's Home".

2 Baker 1969, p. 88, see also p. 67 for an account of the incident of July 8, 1918 to which reference is made here.

3 Cf. Baker 1969, pp. 108–110.

> bankruptcy – you have overdrawn. ... When you have changed your ideas and aims in life, you will find your mother waiting to welcome you, whether it be in this world or the next – loving you and longing for your love. The Good Lord watch between me and thee, while we are absent one from the other.

The letter was signed: "Your still hoping and praying mother Grace Hall Hemingway." Hemingway complained that "he was now literally homeless".[4] As with "The End of Something", biography provides much of the material for this story.[5] Yet it is expanded in "Soldier's Home" into an account of a both typical and specific post-1918 situation.

Analysis

Place names of various kinds mark out the geographical and moral world of Harold Krebs. He comes from a middle-class background in provincial Oklahoma and finishes his schooling "at a Methodist college in Kansas" (**14** 1). Suddenly, in 1917, he volunteers to join the Marines and finds himself in Europe, fighting his way from "Belleau Wood, Soissons, the Champagne, St. Mihiel and ... the Argonne" to the Rhine (**14** 16–17). That Krebs has not managed to cope with this radical displacement is shown with suggestive economy in the second paragraph: "Krebs and the corporal look too big for their uniforms. The German girls are not beautiful. The Rhine does not show in the picture" (**14** 7–9). This photograph, meant to be shown off to the folks back home, exposes only that nothing is well, nothing is as it should be. Similarly, Krebs's self-appraisal (**14** 23–26) does not tally with the impression he makes in his home town on his return. For "he came back much too late" (**14** 11). Through no fault of his own, Krebs is just as much a misfit in post-war Oklahoma as he was on the Rhine.

The homecoming goes wrong. All the old familiar places are familiar no longer. Krebs cannot understand what it is that has changed. Narrating half from within Krebs's mind, half as observer from without, Hemingway presents a puzzled protagonist, faced with "such a complicated world" (**15** 31). It is appropriate to say both of his parents and of the pretty girls he observes in the town that "the world they were in was not the world he was in" (**17** 7). By contrast, he can relate to his younger sister Helen, since she reminds him of his prewar boyhood, including baseball.

---

4 This excerpt of the letter and a little more is given by Baker 1969, p. 109. Hemingway's complaint is reported on p. 110.

5 The name "Harold Krebs" is derived from that of Krebs Friend, a war veteran Hemingway got to know in Chicago in 1920. Cf. Baker 1969, pp. 119 and 198.

His inability to relate is expressed in the paradoxical repetitions in the story and in the kind of dialogues that occur. The repetitions show up Krebs's dilemma: "he liked" yet "he did not like"; "he would have liked ... but he did not want"; "he liked" but "it was not worth it" (**16–17**) passim). Krebs himself cannot resolve these paradoxes, but his interior monologue does culminate in a word that holds a key insight: "That was all a lie" (**16** 26). As one critic points out, "what disorients him is not the truth of war but the lie of the Midwestern view of war."[6] For Krebs, life in his home town involves all kinds of lies. Courting a girl involves lying (**16** 15–16), courting people's interest or admiration involves lying, too, (**14** 19–21) and, in addition, is useless. Knowing and telling the truth makes you feel good (**14** 23–24 and **17** 15) but lying, boasting and intriguing lead to nausea (**14** 21–22, **15** 8). What Krebs "vaguely" wants is uncomplicated companionship without "consequences" (**16** 17–18) and in which he does not have to take the initiative (**16** 31–32). But as the interchapter from *In Our Time* printed on p. 28 shows, that kind of companionship is no help, which explains why Krebs prefers the looks of American girls to those he knew in France and Germany. This puzzled awareness of lying is basically his situation when the action proper starts at **17** 18, almost exactly midway through the story (at line 114 of a total of 247 lines). Hemingway has slowly and carefully prepared the ground for what is now going to happen. He has introduced the psychological setting and key concepts which in the second half are acted out and, for the comprehension of the reader, further defined. This two-part structure, as in "The End of Something", is emphasized by the switch from descriptive narrative and interior monologue in part I to the dialogue, with only a minimum of connecting narrative, in part II.

The structure of "Soldier's Home" can thus be illustrated in a diagram (opposite). The frame of this can be prepared on the blackboard or on a transparency and should be filled in by the students in the course of classroom discussion. Creative exercises like finding headlines and putting questions are tied up with analytical activities like finding key words and determining stylistic and narrative techniques. The *Teaching Notes* amplify this general approach.

The third section of the story (section C in the chart) consists of five dialogues of varying length between Harold and his mother and Harold and his sister Helen, alternating and contrasting. Harold's father remains offstage. It is revealing to compare and analyse the dialogues. What is the

---

6 John J. Roberts, "In Defense of Krebs," *Studies in Short Fiction,* 13 (1976), pp. 515–518, p. 517.

The Structure

part section	I A	 B	II C	 D
lines	**14** 1 – **15** 13	**15** 14 – **17** 17	**17** 18 – **20** 33	**20** 34 – **21** 5
headline	"to war and back"	"such a complicated world"	"brother and son"	"leaving home for good"
key words	lies nausea lost everything	to want to like not worth it	duty pretence/lies love nausea	lies smooth vs. complicated
main narrative technique	interior monologue		dialogue	
questions raised	What has gone wrong? What has Harold lost?	Why doesn't Harold want to get involved? What is he afraid of?	How do H. and his mother communicate? H. and his sister? What is the difference?	Why does Harold leave home? Why avoid his father? and not Helen? What is he going to do now?

relationship between mother and son on the one hand, and brother and sister on the other? To what extent are the dialogues successful acts of communication, to what extent are they failures? How can the failures be accounted for? Even the simplest conversation between two people is a complicated linguistic and social process of negotiating meanings. Everyday exchanges are ritualized so that misunderstandings seldom occur, but speech acts like reproaching, accusing, justifying or excusing are much more difficult. "Part of a speaker's task is to understand his hearers, what they know already, and what they expect and want to hear."[7] Does Mrs Krebs succeed in these tasks? Does she even try? Why is Helen more successful at taking Harold's perspective into account than her mother? Such are the questions raised by these dialogues:

1) **17** 18–31	Mrs Krebs and Harold
2) **17** 33–**18** 2	Harold and Helen
3) **18** 6–8	Mrs Krebs and Harold
4) **18** 9–**19** 1	Helen and Harold, exchange ended by Mrs Krebs
5) **19** 1–**20** 35	Mrs Krebs and Harold

The dialogues between mother and son follow a characteristic pattern. At the beginning of each Mrs Krebs adopts an authoritative, no-nonsense attitude (**17** 19, **18** 6, **19** 1–4). The "I want to talk to Harold" of the fifth dialogue is a thinly veiled threat in the sense of "I've got a bone to pick with you, Harold", and much the same thing is implied by her deliberate gesture of smoothing her apron and by the introductory ploy of "I had a talk with your father last night". Many of her contributions to the dialogues are orders, again disguised as polite requests. Saying something while pretending to say something else is a form of dissimulation, if not of lying. Other contributions by Mrs Krebs are direct and indirect reproaches, the indirect ones, as reports of what the invisible Mr Krebs has said, almost unanswerable. Wholly unanswerable are the reproaches based on scriptural authority (**19** 13–16). Briefly, Mrs Krebs is making demands on her son, while he is trying to escape them. And Harold is the loser, since their relationship is asymmetrical. Mrs Krebs, with her husband, public example (**19** 24–28) and the authority of God to back her, and in her role of tending and caring mother, has all the arguments on her side. Harold, the weak and lazy misfit, has nothing to support him but his sister's affection and the option of flight. There is no home for *this* soldier.

---

7 Michael Stubbs, *Discourse Analysis: The Psycholinguistic Analysis of Natural Language,* Oxford 1983, p. 31.

The Poems

Part II of this reader is prefaced by one of Hemingway's poems and concluded by a poem of Richard Aldington's. Both, different as they are, are written in the tradition of imagism, in that they rely on clear, concrete details and are based on a single image or metaphor. In the case of Hemingway's poem the unifying principle is the personification of time in "the age demanded" and "the age was handed". This pseudo-dialogue, a sequence of demanding and handing the demander what he deserves, inevitably echoes the dialogues between Mrs Krebs and her son. There is no point in pretending that "The Age Demanded" is a great poem[8] – it is rather a specimen of rudely satirical humour and partly, too, a parody of Ezra Pound's "Hugh Selwyn Mauberley" (1915), in which the following lines occur:

> The age demanded an image
> Of its accelerated grimace,
> Something for the modern stage,
> Not, at any rate, an Attic grace.

Hemingway's poem is certainly not a specimen of Attic grace. It does, however, reflect the situation of men like Harold Krebs who are out of harmony with their age and unable to speak up for themselves against it (**13** 2): "And cut away our tongue".

Richard Aldington's "Bombardment" is given here as another man's report on the experience of war. For most teachers and for all students the knowledge of war is vicarious, gained, mercifully, through other men's suffering. In this sense Hemingway, Aldington and Auden (p. 26) are to be seen as witnesses of war, each contributing in their way to our knowledge. This is particularly important for reading "Soldier's Home" because in this story no real description of war is given; that part of the ice-berg is submerged. Harold Krebs's memory of the war, which is gradually obliterated as his first post-war summer passes, was originally "cool and clear" and of doing "the one thing, the only thing for a man to do, easily and naturally" (**14** 23–26). What thing? We are not told. Perhaps we can conclude from **17** 12–17 that Krebs is thinking of the military efficiency of the campaign of July to November 1918, the final battle of World War I. Aldington, by contrast, depicts the soldiers under bombardment as anything but cool and clear. They are helpless, frightened victims of an anonymous artillery attack. All they can do is "sweat and listen" and hope that they will not be hit. The third stanza describes the soldiers' puzzlement that the horror of

8 Baker 1969, p. 203, calls it "puppy doggerel".

such a bombardment has left no trace whatever on the serene beauty of the sky, whereas the earth and they themselves are wrecked. This puzzlement may serve as a clue to understanding Krebs, for even in his story there are hints that the war was not as cool and clear as he would like to remember it. There is an unresolved contradiction between his claim that he had not wanted to come home (**17** 3) and the statement that "now ... things were getting good again" (**17** 11, see also **21** 3–4). Perhaps Krebs, too, experienced something like the bombardment that Aldington writes about? If so, and it is historically likely, Aldington's poem fills in a gap in Krebs's memory, reconstitutes an experience that he has suppressed, and helps to explain why he cannot easily settle down at home.

First Unit: Back Home

Several Hemingway critics have pointed out that one of the basic structures of his fiction is a kind of antithetical movement. Carlos Baker describes this as the tension between "Home" and "Not-Home"[9]. Philip Young believes that there is a recurrent plot pattern of the hero departing from home and returning to the place where he was wounded[10]. In many stories it is the event and the place of being wounded that keep on returning to the hero, haunting him in his weakest moments. The physical wound heals and only a scar remains, but the emotional wound is there for ever. In the case of Harold Krebs the wound of the spirit can only be guessed at from the way he behaves. From the battlegrounds of Europe he has brought home the knowledge of war, of women, of independent and responsible action, but also of unnamed, fearful "consequences". Back home, he senses the difference between himself and the people and places of his home town and cannot bridge the gap. Krebs can look on but not participate.

1. *What kind of place is Krebs's home town? Collect all the information the story gives you.*
15 15: town library
15 15–16: parents' house with front porch
15 18: pool room (presumably attached to a saloon or bar)
15 19: "down town", i. e. business centre of the town
15 28: First National Bank

---

9 Carlos Baker, *Hemingway: The Writer as Artist,* Princeton 1952, pp. 101–102.
10 Young 1952, pp. 5, 25, 190–194.

16 5: tree-shaded streets
16 10: the Greek's ice cream parlor
18 10: Helen's school
Krebs's home town is described through these details as a very average place, very different and distant from the places Krebs got to know in Europe.

2. *Find out about American involvement in World War I, using maps, reference or history books to follow up the information given in **14** 3–5 and **14** 16 – **15** 7.*
This is suggested as homework or as the subject of a brief report by one or more students. All kinds of sources can be used, one teaching objective of such an assignment being to compare and evaluate whatever material happens to be at hand. Useful and easily accessible sources are:
Udo Sautter, *Geschichte der Vereinigten Staaten von Amerika,* Stuttgart 1976 (Kröner), pp. 328–339.
Peter N. Carroll/David W. Noble, *The Free and the Unfree: A New History of the United States,* New York 1977 (Penguin), pp. 310–314.
John A. Garraty, *American History,* New York 1982 (Harcourt Brace Jovanovich; distributed in Germany by Klett, Klettbuch 51615), pp. 676–704.
These are brief accounts; a lot of interesting detail is given by Samuel Eliot Morison in *The Oxford History of the American People,* paperback ed. New York 1972, especially pp. 196–205, with a map of the "American Participation in the Allied Offensive of 1918" on p. 201. As Morison points out, 18 out of the 29 American divisions that saw action in France were composed of volunteers who had undergone a mere eight months of training before seeing action. "The American Expeditionary Force of 1917–18 was a jolly, singing army compared with the grim, tight-lipped American Army of 1942–45. Music and banners were not wanting; New York's tin-pan alley ground out some excellent marching songs such as Irving Berlin's 'Oh, How I Hate to Get Up in the Morning!' Official propaganda aimed to make the A.E.F. feel like knights errant rescuing damsel France from the wicked Hun; . . . 'We cried more over the Americans leaving for the front than over our own men,' said a French peasant woman at a village near the front lines – 'They were so young and looked so innocent, and were so far from home'" (pp. 197–198). Irving Berlin's song is reprinted in Morison p. 221 and there is a contrasting song "I Didn't Raise My Boy to Be a Soldier" on p. 189.

3. *What kind of a welcome does Krebs get when he returns home? In what sense does he come back "much too late" (**14** 11)?*

As is explained on **14** 10–15 there is no elaborate public welcome in the summer of 1919. Europe is distant and the war is past and Midwestern Americans are busy with their everyday lives. No one is interested in hearing war stories any more, no matter how lurid. There are two different patterns of behaviour in Harold's family. Like their fellow-citizens, Mr and Mrs Krebs are not interested (**14** 18, **15** 23). On the other hand, Harold's two sisters admire him and generally sympathize with him (**15** 20, **17** 35–37, **18** 13). Mrs Krebs even suspects that her son's morals have become corrupted by the war (**19** 18–21). Krebs cannot share his experiences with anyone. This might have been easier if he had returned half a year earlier together with all the other soldiers. He also returns too late in that everyday life has resumed its old course, leaving him as an outsider and spectator. His experience of the discrepancy between war in Europe and peace at home is rather like that expressed in the last lines of Aldington's "Bombardment":

> And looked above the wreckage of the earth
> To where the white clouds moved in silent lines
> Across the untroubled blue.

4. *How does Krebs behave at home? What do you think of his behaviour? Can you account for it?*

First he doesn't want to talk, and when he does no one wants to listen (**14** 17–18).
He boasts, exaggerates, tells lies, and finally becomes sick of "everything" (**15** 13), i.e. his experiences in Europe.
He is generally lazy and inactive (**15** 14–20).
He watches the young girls in the street but remains wholly passive (**15** 30 – **17** 11).
He is aggressive towards his mother (**17** 22, 26).
He is friendly with Helen (**17** 37 – **18** 33).
He feels "embarrassed and resentful" (**19** 17) towards his mother, then "sick and vaguely nauseated" (**20** 23) and finally sorry for her (**20** 36–37).

Although his mother doesn't understand him, Harold's behaviour is perfectly natural. He needs time to come to terms with the experience of war, of being away from home, of German and French girls. He cannot simply behave as if nothing had happened. He cannot adopt his mother's rigorous puritanical standards of work and morals, even though they formed the basis of his education (**14** 1). Also, his mother behaves aggressively towards him, so he only answers back in kind (**17** 20, cf. p. 46 above).

Second Unit: Reconstituting the Dialogues

We have seen that the second half of this story consists mainly of dialogues and that the dialogues between Harold and his mother do not lead to successful communication. Neither of them completely knows, understands or accepts the assumptions and intentions underlying the other's speeches. As each dialogue proceeds they neither speak honestly in their own persons nor do they react honestly to the speech of their partner. Instead of trying to negotiate a message acceptable to both they take any opportunity to lash out at each other. The formula is mutual distrust. How the dialogues work has in part been discussed on p. 46 above. The aim of this unit is to let the students work out in detail how the non-communication takes place and to try to reconstitute the faulty dialogues, i.e. suggest how they could be rewritten to work properly. In this way, analysis and language production can be combined. A more general aim is to demonstrate that non-communication can be traced to overt and covert aggressiveness and that conversely peaceful communication is achieved through adopting consciously certain attitudes and using language in a certain way. A theoretical basis for such an approach is supplied by Martin Buber's concept of dialogue.[11]

1. *How do Harold and his mother talk to each other in the first dialogue narrated to us on **17**?*
The structure of the dialogue can be worked out with the aid of a simple diagram (see p. 52). Such a diagram helps to show up the tactics employed by both speakers.

In her first three speeches, Mrs Krebs does not speak in her own person. Instead she refers to an absent authority. We can safely assume that in fact it is the mother who is the authority in the Krebs home – that would be in keeping with the dominance of mothers in American society.[12] So she is hiding behind the pretended authority of the father. Since Harold receives no responsible, personally authenticated answer, he can only go on repeating his doubts. In this way no progress whatever is made in the dialogue. Harold is all the time saying, in effect, "I don't believe you, and I don't believe father means what you say he said."

---

11 Wilfried Brusch, "Pädagogischer Dialog und echtes Gespräch: James Thurbers 'The Secret Life of Walter Mitty'," *Englisch Amerikanische Studien,* 6 (1984), Heft 3, pp. 415–428, applies Martin Buber's concept of dialogue to EFL.

12 Cf. the section *For Further Study* p. 57 and the reference to Geoffrey Gorer on women in American society.

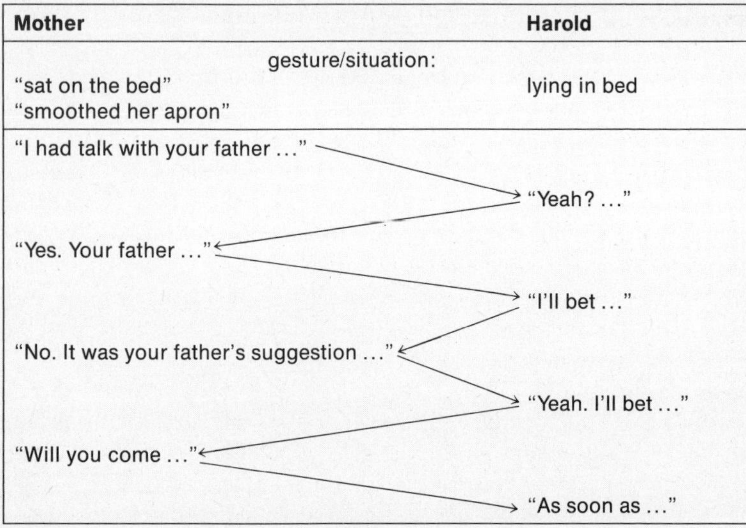

Mrs Krebs, though recognizing this, makes no effort to understand Harold's doubts, nor does she frankly explain what it is she herself really wants her son to do. For Harold recognizes that there must be some ulterior motive to her offer (of the use of father's car) and rebels against the insincerity. This brings us to the next question:

2. *What is Mrs Krebs's intention in offering Harold the use of the car?*
The students are likely to suggest a number of answers here. Closest to Hemingway's text will be those answers based on **19** 31 – **20** 2, in which Mrs Krebs's motives become apparent. She is practically proposing a deal. If Harold promises to "settle down to work" like Charley Simmons (**19** 24–28, 35) and, like other young men of his age, to get interested in "nice girls" then he will be allowed to use the car. "Freedom" and fun must be earned. A more general answer would be that Mrs Krebs is trying to win her son back to the Protestant work ethic. This idea is further explored in Unit 4.

3. *How is this conversation brought to an end?*
In **17** 29 Mrs Krebs abruptly switches to a different subject. It is typical of her way of talking to her son that she uses a "polite" imperative for this purpose. And Harold, of course, gives a cheeky answer (cheeky because it falsely implies that his mother expects him to come to breakfast in pyjamas).

It should be clear from such an analysis that Harold and his mother will not be able to solve his problems together. By contrast, the dialogues with

Helen show how mutual tolerance, speaking to each other as equals and no attempt by one partner to boss the other leads to a relaxed, friendly atmosphere.

The next stage is to try to rewrite the "unsuccessful" dialogues, i.e. to make them communicatively successful. Dialogue no. 1 can be dealt with in class, dialogue no. 2 set for homework. Although this is essentially oral work, it may be too difficult (and perhaps has not been practised) to be done spontaneously in class. So preparatory group work is recommended, with an assignment such as this:

4. *Rewrite dialogue no. 1 as it might take place between father and son. Let Harold accept his father's offer of the use of the car. Let Mr Krebs suggest that the two of them might go on a fishing trip together.*
Obviously this means changing Hemingway's story out of all recognition. There is no sacrilege in this. Rather, the students will be able to judge Hemingway's intentions and achievement all the better by comparing their own versions with the original. The new dialogue should be kept short and simple. Possible version:

One evening at supper, after he had been home about a month, his father pushed his empty plate away from him, lit a cigarette, and turned to Harold.

"Listen Harold," he said, "wouldn't you like to take the car out in the evenings once in a while? I don't usually need it myself in the evenings."

"Huh, why not? That'd be a good idea," said Krebs. He was surprised though.

"Yeah, you can have it. Just let me know in the mornings."

"O. K. Thanks. What about this evening?"

"That's all right with me. Here are the keys. You won't need to fill her up."

"Thanks, Pa," Krebs said. (Etc.)

5. *Rewrite dialogue no. 5, (**19** 1 – **20** 35) trying to rid it of all aggression and intentional or unintentional misunderstandings.*
Possible version:

"Could I ask you something, Harold, when you've finished with the paper?" she said.

"Sure, I've finished, Mom. What's up?"

"Well, I'm worried about your future, Harold. Have you got any ideas about what kind of work you'd like to do, now that you're settling down again?" said Mrs Krebs.

"I haven't thought about it much yet. But why are you worrying?"

"That's difficult to say. I'd like you to be doing something, getting on in life, now that the war is over and you've mercifully returned home safe and sound. Perhaps your father could find a job for you in the real estate business, if you're interested."

"The trouble is that I'm not sure myself yet. You don't need to push me, though – I'm sure I'll find something sooner or later. You know, it's harder to settle down again than you might think."

Mrs Krebs sighed. "Well, perhaps you're right. But do tell us if we can help you. If you want the car, for instance, or if you need father's help. Perhaps the two of you should have a talk. What do you think?"

"O. K., suits me. I was thinking of seeing a friend in Kansas City, a guy I know from the army. I could do with the car for that, Mom."

"Well, just tell your father when you need it."

The students will probably come to the conclusion, when they try to work out their own versions, that the second part of the original dialogue, from **20** 4 to **20** 35, will no longer be necessary. Mrs Krebs will not need to employ emotional blackmail if she and her son come to an understanding. It should be made quite clear in class that the exercise proposed here in no way aims to "improve" Hemingway. Its aim is rather to show by contrast how the original text functions – and to get in a bit of language practice as well.

A further (or alternative) opportunity for language production is provided by **20** 9–12. Here Hemingway employs the characteristic indeterminate "it" and "something" again, prompting a question like:

6. *What is it Harold can't tell his mother? Why? What is it he is angry at?*

Third Unit: The Disharmony of Roles and Standards

As has already been pointed out, the values of Harold's Methodist upbringing have been eroded by the initiatory experience of the war in Europe. Mrs Krebs's standards, on the other hand, seem never to have been challenged. Both to Harold and to the reader they appear as firm, inflexible, even rigid. If the army has taught Harold some things (**16** 19, 27, 30), it has not prepared him for civilian life and for the responsibilities of adulthood. The long section from **15** 30 to **17** 17, i. e. section B, shows that Harold has lost contact with those people who were his peer group two years earlier. Now he neither dares nor has the energy (**15** 32) to renew the contact. His contemporaries, like Charley Simmons, are a long step ahead of him. The only times Harold meets with approval is when he reverts to childhood standards, as in his relations with Helen, and with his mother (**20** 21–24). Harold is incapable of playing any role in which he could be in harmony with the set-up in his family and in his home town. The linguistic aspect of this disharmony has been looked into in Unit Two. This Unit inquires into the values and standards that differentiate the characters and provide the ideological basis for disharmony.

1. *Read through the story again and make a list of the virtues and vices that are invoked by the different characters. How do your findings affect your interpretation of the characters?*
The first part of this is a homework assignment. It can result in a chart like the following:

	VIRTUES	VICES
Harold	a good soldier (**14** 25, **17** 17) honesty (**15** 8–9, (**20** 29–31) affection (**17** 37, **18** 16–29, **21** 5)	lying and boasting (**15** 8–9; **20** 37)
Helen	affection (cf. Harold)	
Mrs Krebs	ambition (**19** 24) aim in life (**19** 24) determination to get somewhere (**19** 26) being a credit to the community (**19** 27–28) love (**19** 30, **20** 4ff.) faith (**19** 13–16, 21; **20** 25–34) obedience (**20** 24) work (**19** 35–36)	disorder (**18** 6–7) idleness (**19** 14) (sexual) temptation (**19** 19)

Harold expresses or shows only a few moral attitudes but is consistent about them. Honesty is his main positive attribute, fear of responsibility his main negative one. Helen's function in the story is to show what kind of affection Harold is capable of, so only this virtue is linked with her. Mrs Krebs is the most complex of the three: she demonstrates or invokes a mixture of religious, ethic and socio-economic attitudes. She uses positive values like love, filial obedience and "enjoyment" (**19** 34) to exert pressure on Harold. This tends to discredit the purity and disinterestedness of such values, especially since Harold understands the invocation of love and work as a form of the devious intrigue that he recoils from (**16** 14).

The teacher can go on from here to introduce the concept of the Puritan (or Protestant) work ethic (cf. *For Further Study*, p. 57).

2. *What is meant by "love" in this short story? Distinguish between different characters' use of the word.*
For Helen (and for Harold when he is talking to her) the word is used playfully to mean "mutual sympathy", "affection" or "playing at being in love". For Mrs Krebs the term has a negative and two positive meanings. As a part of getting married and, preparatory to that, taking out the "nice girls" (**19** 25, 33) it is acceptable. Its darker side, "sin", is not expressed but just alluded to (**19** 19–21) and perhaps there is even a hint of original sin, passed on from one generation to the next. The other positive meaning, positive at least from Mrs Krebs's point of view, is "maternal love" (**20** 21–22), though for Harold (and for the reader) it is nauseating. Harold's own attitude to love is ambivalent. He remembers casual, uncomplicated and irresponsible sexual encounters during the war as pleasant: "It was simple and you were friends" (**16** 35 – **17** 1). The girls at home are more attractive (**17** 6), perhaps because ethically more acceptable given the standards of Harold's upbringing, but he is put off by the complicated rituals of courtship which are demanded at home. So he accepts love in the innocent sense embodied by Helen and in the sexual sense, but rejects his mother's versions. Harold's attitude is comparable to that of the Roman soldier in Auden's "Roman Wall Blues" (**26**).

3. *Does Harold, in the course of the story, make any kind of progress in understanding himself and his situation? Comment especially on **20** 36.*
– Yes. He gradually comes to understand that there is no home for him in his home town, that he does not fit, and that his parents' standards are not his. "None of it had touched him" means that he is proud of having maintained his independence in spite of his mother's attempts to reintegrate him. He gradually comes to understand what is different between himself and his mother and so rejects her and his home.
– No. At the end of the story he runs away from a situation which is too complicated for him to understand and handle. He has not matured at all, either morally or intellectually. He rejects his home because he does not understand it.

The following supplementary question again provides the opportunity for creative writing based on reading inferences.

4. *"There would be one more scene maybe before he got away"* (**21** *1–2*). *What kind of scene is Harold thinking of? Describe what you think this scene is going to be like.*
Harold means a final quarrel with his mother, which may take much the same course as dialogue no. 5. But this time, perhaps, he will not recant on a statement like "I don't love anybody".

The students' version may be done as direct speech, indirect report or interior monologue ("Two days later Krebs got on board the train for Kansas City. He did not look back as the train pulled out of the station. This time he had told her. He had not felt sorry and he had not lied. ...").

For Further Study

Mrs Krebs is a figure who could easily be misunderstood, especially by non-native readers, as a hypocrite or as the satirical portrait of a Puritan. It may be useful, therefore, to give the students a supplementary background text to read.

The following text is taken from Geoffrey Gorer, *The American People: A Study in National Character,* New York 1948 (Norton), pp. 54–56:

> In few societies is the role of the father more vestigial than in the United States. [...] The fact that the American mother has arrogated to herself, or has had thrust upon her, the dominant role in the rearing of her children [...] has far-reaching results on the character of the children. [...] The means by which a moral character [...] is formed is now fairly well understood. [...] Parents (or parent substitutes) train children to an ethical viewpoint by giving love and rewards when the children conform to arbitrary moral standards, and withdrawing love and inflicting punishment when the children fail to conform. By the process of anticipation the children learn to act toward those moral standards as if the parents were present. [...] This internalized control becomes part of the total personality; it is called by the psychoanalysts the superego, in common speech the conscience.
>
> The idiosyncratic feature of the American conscience is that it is predominantly feminine. Owing to the major role played by the mother in disciplining the child, in rewarding and punishing it, many more aspects of the mother than of the father become incorporated. Duty and Right Conduct become feminine figures.
>
> This makes the role of the daughter, herself to become a mother, particularly easy and straightforward, and helps account for the perpetuation of the situation. [...] But for the son, the American male, the situation is far more complicated and confusing. He carries around, as it were encapsulated inside him, an ethical, admonitory, censorious mother. In all the spheres where moral considerations are meant to operate – and in America this means above all in relations between people – men act as though they were being guided by (or rebelling against) rules and prohibitions enunciated by a moral mother.

Alternatively, the students can be asked to read and report on the whole of Chapter II of Gorer's book, from which the above excerpt is taken, in the German translation, which is perhaps more readily available: Geoffrey Gorer, *Die Amerikaner: Eine völkerpsychologische Studie,* Hamburg 1956 (Rowohlt, rde 9).

A film version of "Soldier's Home" is available on video cassette from the Institut für Film und Bild in Wissenschaft und Unterricht (FWU), Bavaria-Film-Platz 3, 8022 Grünwald, or on loan through the local "Bildstelle" or "Amerika Haus". The order no. is 41/42 0143. There is a useful leaflet accompanying the 37 minute film version with information and didactic hints particularly on the differences between text and film. The film should not be shown before the story has been read and discussed in class. The complete screenplay (film script), written by Robert Geller, is printed in Calvin Skaggs, ed., *The American Short Story,* Vol. 1, New York 1977 (Dell-Laurel Books 1979). The script is a complete rewriting of Hemingway's story, introducing new scenes, characters and motives. As Arthur Waldhorn comments: "The film versions distort or evade Hemingway's vision of experience."[13] On the use of the film in the classroom, see Horst Groene and Günter Schubert, "Hemingways 'Soldier's Home' als Short Story und Film im fortgeschrittenen Englischunterricht," *Der fremdsprachliche Unterricht,* 19, Heft 73 (Feb. 1985), pp. 3–9.

A general aim of this kind of course is to get students interested in reading further books for themselves. So the teacher could point out that Erich Maria Remarque's *Im Westen nichts Neues* (1929) describes experiences that in many respects parallel those of Nick Adams and Harold Krebs. One could discuss, for example, if Remarque's brief preface applies to Krebs: "Dieses Buch soll weder eine Anklage noch ein Bekenntnis sein. Es soll nur den Versuch machen, über eine Generation zu berichten, die vom Kriege zerstört wurde – auch wenn sie seinen Granaten entkam." In chapter VII, the hero of the novel, Paul, is on leave. He reports: "Ich finde mich hier nicht mehr zurecht, es ist eine fremde Welt. Die einen fragen, die anderen fragen nicht, und man sieht ihnen an, daß sie stolz darauf sind; oft sagen sie es sogar noch mit dieser Miene des Verstehens, daß man darüber nicht reden könne. Sie bilden sich etwas darauf ein." (Frankfurt/Berlin 1966, Ullstein Buch 56, p. 121).

13 Arthur Waldhorn, *A Reader's Guide to Ernest Hemingway,* New York 1972, p. 265. The book contains a filmography, pp. 265–266.

PART III

Today Is Friday

Three Roman soldiers are in a drinking-place at eleven o'clock at night. There are barrels around the wall. Behind the wooden counter is a Hebrew wine-seller. The three Roman soldiers are a little cock-eyed.

1st Soldier – You tried the red?

2nd Soldier – No, I ain't tried it.

1st Soldier – You better try it.

2nd Soldier – All right, George, we'll have a round of the red.

Hebrew Wine-seller – Here you are, gentlemen. You'll like that. [*He sets down an earthenware pitcher that he has filled from one of the casks.*] That's a nice little wine.

1st Soldier – Have a drink of it yourself. [*He turns to the third Roman soldier who is leaning on a barrel.*] What's the matter with you?

3rd Soldier – I got a gut-ache.

2nd Soldier – You've been drinking water.

1st Soldier – Try some of the red.

3rd Soldier – I can't drink the damn stuff. It makes my gut sour.

1st Soldier – You been out here too long.

3rd Soldier – Hell, don't I know it?

1st Soldier – Say, George, can't you give this gentleman something to fix up his stomach?

Wine-seller – I got it right here.

[*The third Roman soldier tastes the cup that the wine-seller has mixed for him.*]

3rd Soldier – Hey, what you put in that, camel chips?

2 **barrel** round wooden container for wine, etc. – **Hebrew** [ˈhi:bru:] – 3 **cock-eyed** *slang* drunk – 9 **pitcher** large jug – 13 **gut-ache** [ˈgʌteɪk] stomach-ache – 24 **camel chips** pieces of dried camel dung used as fuel

Wine-seller – You drink that right down, Lootenant. That'll fix you up right.

3rd Soldier – Well, I couldn't feel any worse.

1st Soldier – Take a chance on it. George fixed me up fine the other day.

Wine-seller – You were in bad shape, Lootenant. I know what fixes up a bad stomach.

[*The third Roman soldier drinks the cup down.*]

3rd Soldier – Jesus Christ. [*He makes a face.*]

2nd Soldier – That false alarm!

1st Soldier – Oh, I don't know. He was pretty good in there today.

2nd Soldier – Why didn't he come down off the cross?

1st Soldier – He didn't want to come down off the cross. That's not his play.

2nd Soldier – Show me a guy that doesn't want to come down off the cross.

1st Soldier – Aw, hell, you don't know anything about it. Ask George there. Did he want to come down off the cross, George?

Wine-seller – I'll tell you, gentlemen, I wasn't out there. It's a thing I haven't taken any interest in.

2nd Soldier – Listen, I seen a lot of them – here and plenty of other places. Any time you show me one that doesn't want to get down off the cross when the time comes – when the time comes, I mean – I'll climb right up with him.

1st Soldier – I thought he was pretty good in there today.

3rd Soldier – He was all right.

2nd Soldier – You guys don't know what I'm talking about. I'm not saying whether he was good or not. What I mean is, when the time comes. When they first start nailing him, there isn't none of them wouldn't stop it if they could.

1st Soldier – Didn't you follow it, George?

Wine-seller – No, I didn't take any interest in it, Lootenant.

1st Soldier – I was surprised how he acted.

3rd Soldier – The part I don't like is the nailing them on. You know, that must get to you pretty bad.

2nd Soldier – It isn't that that's so bad, as when they first lift 'em up. [*He makes a lifting gesture with his two palms together.*] When the weight starts

1 **lootenant** lieutenant; phonetic spelling of *AE* [lu:ˈtenənt] as opposed to *BE* [lefˈtenənt] – 34 **that must get to you** that is sure to affect you – 36 **palm** inside surface of the hand

to pull on 'em. That's when it gets 'em.

3rd Soldier – It takes some of them pretty bad.

1st Soldier – Ain't I seen 'em? I seen plenty of them. I tell you, he was pretty good in there today.

[*The second Roman soldier smiles at the Hebrew wine-seller.*]

2nd Soldier – You're a regular Christer, big boy.

1st Soldier – Sure, go on and kid him. But listen while I tell you something. He was pretty good in there today.

2nd Soldier – What about some more wine?

[*The wine-seller looks up expectantly. The third Roman soldier is sitting with his head down. He does not look well.*]

3rd Soldier – I don't want any more.

2nd Soldier – Just for two, George.

[*The wine-seller puts out a pitcher of wine, a size smaller than the last one. He leans forward on the wooden counter.*]

1st Soldier – You see his girl?

2nd Soldier – Wasn't I standing right by her?

1st Soldier – She's a nice-looker.

2nd Soldier – I knew her before he did. [*He winks at the wine-seller.*]

1st Soldier – I used to see her around the town.

2nd Soldier – She used to have a lot of stuff. He never brought *her* no good luck.

1st Soldier – Oh, he ain't lucky. But he looked pretty good to me in there today.

2nd Soldier – What become of his gang?

1st Soldier – Oh, they faded out. Just the women stuck by him.

2nd Soldier – They were a pretty yellow crowd. When they seen him go up there they didn't want any of it.

1st Soldier – The women stuck all right.

2nd Soldier – Sure, they stuck all right.

1st Soldier – You see me slip the old spear into him?

2nd Soldier – You'll get into trouble doing that some day.

1st Soldier – It was the least I could do for him. I'll tell you he looked pretty good to me in there today.

6 **Christer** [ˈkraɪstə] – 7 **to kid s. o.** to make fun of s. o.. to pull s. o.'s leg – 26 **to fade out** to disappear, to leave – 27 **yellow** *slang* cowardly – 29 **to stick** to stay (with s. o.)

Wine-seller – Gentlemen, you know I got to close.

1st Soldier – We'll have one more round.

2nd Soldier – What's the use? This stuff don't get you anywhere. Come on, let's go.

1st Soldier – Just another round.

3rd Soldier – [*Getting up from the barrel.*] No, come on. Let's go. I feel like hell tonight.

1st Soldier – Just one more.

2nd Soldier – No, come on. We're going to go. Good-night, George. Put it on the bill.

Wine-seller – Good-night, gentlemen. [*He looks a little worried.*] You couldn't let me have a little something on account, Lootenant?

2nd Soldier – What the hell, George! Wednesday's payday.

Wine-seller – It's all right, Lootenant. Good-night, gentlemen.

[*The three Roman soldiers go out the door into the street.*]

[*Outside in the street.*]

2nd Soldier – George is a kike just like all the rest of them.

1st Soldier – Oh, George is a nice fella.

2nd Soldier – Everybody's a nice fella to you tonight.

3rd Soldier – Come on, let's go up to the barracks. I feel like hell tonight.

2nd Soldier – You been out here too long.

3rd Soldier – No, it ain't just that. I feel like hell.

2nd Soldier – You been out here too long. That's all.

CURTAIN

17 **kike** [kaɪk] *vulgar* Jew – 18 **fella** phonetic spelling of fellow

Roman Wall Blues

Over the heather the wet wind blows,
I've lice in my tunic and a cold in my nose.

The rain comes pattering out of the sky,
I'm a Wall soldier, I don't know why.

The mist creeps over the hard grey stone,
My girl's in Tungria; I sleep alone.

Aulus goes hanging around her place,
I don't like his manners, I don't like his face.

Piso's a Christian, he worships a fish;
There'd be no kissing if he had his wish.

She gave me a ring but I diced it away;
I want my girl and I want my pay.

When I'm a veteran with only one eye
I shall do nothing but look at the sky.

2 **lice** pl. of *louse* small insect living as a parasite on the bodies of people – 6 **Tungria** part of the Roman province of Gallia Belgica – 9 **he worships a fish** the fish was used as a symbol of Christ by the early Christians because the letters of its Greek name formed a monogram of the initial letters of the words Jesus Christ – 11 **to dice s.th. away** to lose s.th. at playing dice (beim Würfeln verlieren)

Interpretation and Teaching Notes

Background

Hemingway's parents were not very pleased with their son in the years 1926 and 1927. Ernest's first real novel, *The Sun Also Rises,* was published in 1926, selling well and finding favour with most of the critics. But for Grace Hemingway it was "one of the filthiest books of the year" and she wrote to ask her son if he had "ceased to be interested in loyalty, nobility and honour."[1] On the face of it, "Today Is Friday" looks like being just the kind of work to corroborate Mrs Hemingway's verdict. Even Carlos Baker describes it as "the tasteless little account of the aftermath of the Crucifixion."[2]

The writing of "Today Is Friday" coincided with a critical period in Hemingway's life. On January 27, 1927 he was divorced from Hadley and on May 10 married Pauline Pfeiffer in Paris. Pauline was a Catholic, and throughout 1926 Ernest had been fumbling his way back to the Catholic faith – "back" because in 1918 "he had been 'baptized in the faith by a priest who had walked between the aisles of wounded men' in an Italian dressing station." He described himself as a "very dumb Catholic."[3]

Analysis

Even if the language of "Today Is Friday" is vulgar and the characters are mean, does not some of the momentousness of the event behind the scene "filter" through the soldiers' conversation? Without knowing it, without at all understanding it, these Roman soliders have just been eyewitnesses of an event which, to look at it honestly, has always been beyond people's understanding. Whereas each of us readers of the story has been provided with some kind of interpretation of Christ's death through education, tradition and faith, the contemporaries presented by Hemingway are so close to the event, so unprepared for it that they can come to a sense of it only on the level of their direct, unaided experience. The three soldiers are, to quote Harold Krebs, "not of His Kingdom" – how could they be? It does not

1 Baker 1962, p. 273.
2 Baker 1962, p. 488. Most critics agree.
3 Baker 1962, p. 281.

matter that the words they find for their experience are primitive as long as they are honest words.

As in the two previous stories, the ability to speak honestly about something beyond understanding is one of Hemingway's central themes. The soldiers can talk accurately only of the technicalities of death by crucifixion, in much the same way as Nick can talk about fishing. But at least one of them, the third soldier, and perhaps the first soldier as well, has an inkling that there is more to this Jesus than to all those other people they have seen executed. What the story shows, then, is the gradual and only partial perception of a deeper significance. It will be for the reader to see if he is capable of putting his sense of the meaning of Christ's death into more coherent words, ideally into words that are authentically personal. In this way Hemingway's ice-berg technique again encourages the students to express themselves.

Although the story is presented on the page as a dramatic scene there is nothing intrinsically dramatic about it.[4] The presentation has the advantage of saving Hemingway an endless repetition of "the first soldier said" or "the other soldier said". It also does away with unnecessary padding between the passages of direct speech. Perhaps a further advantage is the greater immediacy of the present tense as used in the stage directions.

Like a classical drama, however, the story observes the unities of time, place and action. The action begins at eleven o'clock and can be assumed to end at midnight. The three drunken, melancholy soldiers gradually drift into talking about their business of the day and then gradually lose track of the subject again. No one enters or leaves the tavern. There are no scene divisions but a kind of five-part structure with a rising and a falling action. The central section is that of the thematic climax and is introduced by the third soldier's anachronistic swearing "Jesus Christ". Parts two and four are each introduced by a question which turns the conversation on to a new

---

4 Arthur Waldhorn regards "Today Is Friday" as an example of Hemingway's inability to write in the dramatic form, cf. *A Reader's Guide to Ernest Hemingway,* New York 1972, pp. 88–89. Suggestions on teaching this short story and on its suitability for performance are made by Rolf Högel, "'Today is Friday': Eine religiöse dramatische Szene von Ernest Hemingway im Englischunterricht", *Praxis des Neusprachlichen Unterrichts,* 24 (1977), pp. 41–46. Cf. also the interpretation by Friedhelm Güntert, "Zum Thema der Kreuzigung in Hemingway's Einakter 'Today is Friday'", *Die Neueren Sprachen,* 21 (1972), pp. 538–543, which suggests a different interpretation of the second soldier than that proposed here.

subject, i. e. **22** 12, "What's the matter with you?", and **24** 16, "You see his girl?" Parts one and five are the opening and closing scenes, ordering a new round of wine and leaving after the last one. This can be represented in a clock-face diagram:

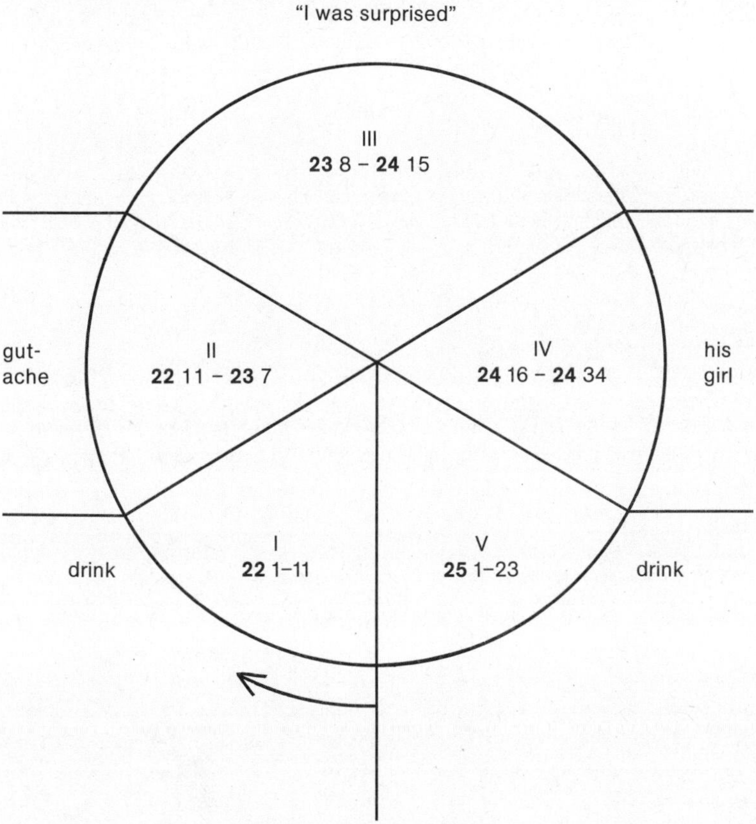

The left half of the clock-face represents the rising action, the slow working round of not particularly acute minds to the subject that at bottom is occupying their thoughts. This culminates in the 1st soldier's admission that the crucifixion has affected him in some way: "I was surprised how he acted" (**23** 32). This can be seen as an indication that he is moved by what he has witnessed, just as in Matthew 27:54 the soldiers "feared greatly, saying, 'Truly this was the Son of God!'" In the same way the third soldier's "gut-ache" is not due to too much drink or to homesickness, but to a feeling of sympathy for the crucified Jew. In other words, a process of conversion has begun, and it is in this sense that one of the earlier titles for the story was "One More For the Nazarene". William James (the brother of the novelist Henry James) cites in his *The Varieties of Religious Experience* the conversion of an alcoholic in New York in the 1890s as an instance of a spiritual rebirth where the convert does not initially understand what has caused it. It is the case of S. H. Hadley who tells his story thus:

> One Tuesday evening I sat in a saloon in Harlem, a homeless, friendless, dying drunkard. I had pawned or sold everything that would bring a drink. I could not sleep unless I was dead drunk. I had not eaten for days, and for four nights preceding I had suffered with delirium tremens, or the horrors, from midnight till morning. I had often said, 'I will never be a tramp. I will never be cornered, for when the time comes, if it ever comes, I will find a home in the bottom of the river.' But the Lord so ordered it that when that time did come I was not able to walk one quarter of the way to the river. As I sat there thinking, I seemed to feel some great and mighty presence. I did not know then what it was. I did learn afterwards that it was Jesus, the sinner's friend.[5]

Perhaps the Roman soldiers, too, will "learn afterwards that it was Jesus, the sinner's friend," and indeed this would be the logical future extension of the story that Hemingway, characteristically, does not spell out. Instead, a falling action, represented by the right half of the clock-face, leads away again from the still nine-tenths submerged theme. In part four, two of the soldiers talk about Mary Magdalene and the first soldier mentions how he stabbed Christ with his spear. The third soldier, the one who is closest to conversion, has fallen silent again. The final part of the story returns to the level of part one, so that the soldiers' mental focus can now be said to have come full circle. This circularity is confirmed by the almost monotonous repetition and variation of just a few key phrases and exclamations. Some of these express the soldiers' limited mental and linguistic powers (e.g. the repetition of "fix up" in **22** 19, **23** 1,4 and 5). The repetition of others is emphatically suggestive of a meaning below the surface, as the breakdown of comments on Jesus in part three may show (see p. 69).

The three Roman soldiers and the Jewish landlord represent four distinct points of view. The first soldier admires Jesus' courage, the second doubts that there is anything to admire, the third is physically and morally

5 William James, *The Varieties of Religious Experience: A Study in Human Nature* (1901–2), Glasgow 1977 (Fountain Books, Fontana).

Sequence of judgements on Jesus in Part III

No.	1st soldier	2nd soldier	3rd soldier	wine-seller
1			Jesus Christ	
2		that false alarm		
3	I don't know/ pretty good			
4	not his play			
5		show me a guy that doesn't		
6	you don't know anything			
7				haven't taken any interest
8		show me one that doesn't		
9	pretty good			
10			all right	
11		there isn't one who wouldn't		
12				didn't take any interest
13	I was surprised			
14			that must get to you pretty bad	
15		that's when it gets them		
16			takes some of them pretty bad	
17	pretty good			
18		you're a regular Christer		
19	pretty good			
20			[*He does not look well.*]	

overwhelmed by the afternoon's events. The cautious landlord claims to be not interested. Whereas the second soldier derides Jesus as "that false alarm", both the first and the third soldiers feel some kind of sympathy or involvement. Their way of talking about him is parallel: the first soldier calls his "performance" "pretty good", the third conjectures that his sufferings must have been "pretty bad". In comparing the two points of view, one could argue that the first soldier's concern with Jesus is more superficial, and his conversion to that extent imperfect, while the third soldier's reaction, though not so articulate, is more deeply felt.

A noticeable feature of the soldiers' language is their use of swear-words. The use of exclamations like "hell" (**22** 18, **23** 16, **25** 7, 13, 20, 22), "damn" (**22** 16) and "Jesus Christ" (**23** 8) by non-Christians in 30 A. D. is surely not blasphemous in the sense that it would have been at a later date in the history of Christianity. Here it is rather a form of unconscious self-revelation, for the third soldier especially. Without really knowing it, he feels as if he were condemned to hell for what he has done and as if the wine, far from being blessed as it is in other Christian contexts, were an instrument of his damnation. This is the deeper meaning of the third soldier's triple repetition of "I feel like hell" in the final part of the story.[6] The second soldier's "What the hell" (**25** 13) is by contrast a meaningless vulgar swear-word.

While there is of course no Biblical precedent for the tavern scene, there are a number of references to the Roman soldiers in the Gospels. The main passages are:

Matthew 27:	39–44	Jesus mocked cf. **23** 11
	54	reaction of centurion (1st soldier?) and other soldiers to Jesus' death
	55	Mary Magdalene
Mark 15:	29–32	Jesus mocked
	39	reaction of the centurion
	40	Mary Magdalene
Luke 23:	35–39	Jesus mocked
	47	reaction of the centurion
John 19:	34	the soldier with the spear

6 The students might like to discuss a dissenting view like Waldhorn's: "the dialogue is absurdly anachronistic. The problem is not one of irreverence but of irrelevance. Worst of all, feeling 'like hell' – so moving when Nick or Jake Barnes says it – is, in this inadequately motivated blackout skit, woefully insufficient" (Waldhorn 1972, p. 89).

First Unit: Points of View

The purpose of this unit is to identify and compare the different points of view on the crucifixion presented in the story or implied by it. As we have seen, the four characters represent four different attitudes. A further point of view which is implied in the story is the Biblical version of the story. Yet a different point of view is the attitude of each individual reader: "What does Jesus' crucifixion mean to me, how does it affect me today?"

1. *What events have preceded this scene in the tavern?*
This gives the students the opportunity to retell the story of the crucifixion in their own words and as they remember it.

2. *How would you distinguish between the three soldiers' reactions to the day's events?*
As the reactions are gradually disclosed through the five parts of the story this question can best be answered with the aid of the structure diagram on p. 67, filling the labelling in as the discussion progresses. The students can also be asked to try to characterize the soldiers and the landlord ("interested in money", "interested in girls", "sensitive and emotional", etc.).

3. *What do the four characters think of Jesus?*
This is the central question and the subject of the central scene of the story (cf. the diagram p. 69).

4. *Identify the swear-words used by the soldiers. Who uses which of them? What do the swear-words mean to the soldiers and what do they mean to you?*
Cf. p. 70. This assignment is to be dealt with in three separate parts.

5. *Look up the Biblical versions of the story of the crucifixion in an English language edition of the gospels.*
This is a homework assignment. It is suggested that it should not take place before the discussion of questions 1–4. The classroom discussion needs to make use of the tension between, on the one hand, one's unthinking everyday assumptions about the significance of the crucifixion and, on the other hand, the realization on rereading the gospel accounts that there is much that one does not fully understand in them. The Roman soldiers are both models and extreme instances of such partial understanding.

Second Unit: The Meaning of the Experience

1. *An earlier title for the story was "One More for the Nazarene". Which of the soldiers do you think the "one" refers to? Explain.*
As discussed above, the reference is most probably to the third soldier, but perhaps the first soldier will not be far behind. Both are beginning to learn the meaning of Christianity.

2. *Another alternative title was "The Seed of the Church". What interpretation of the story does this suggest?*
"Seed" is a metaphor for the growing of the Church out of small and unlikely beginnings.

3. *Why do you think did Hemingway finally settle for "Today Is Friday" as the title?*
There are all sorts of answers to this. If you compare the three titles then it is clear that this is the most low-key, the least literary, which suits Hemingway's language preferences. More important, the "today" is suggestively ambiguous. It is the present from the point of view of the actors in the dramatic scene. It is also the present from the reader's point of view, a permanent present. There is a similar extension to the reader here as in the title of "A Way You'll Never Be".

4. *Has reading Hemingway's story changed or deepened your understanding of the crucifixion?*
It becomes clear through the story that Jesus is appealing to everyone, even those who took part in killing him, to follow his teaching. Hemingway also suggests that learning to accept Christ's teaching is a process and possibly a painful one. Conversion will be more rapid for some than for others, and for yet others it will not take place at all. And some people will not understand other people's reaction to Christ, as demonstrated in the second soldier's obtuse non-explanation in the last line.

It depends very much on the make-up of each individual class what kind of personal statements this discussion can lead to. A question like "Say what you think Jesus' crucifixion means" should, evidently, be avoided. So "No" is a legitimate answer to question 4.

For Further Study

1. Reading Auden's "Roman Wall Blues" may well be left to the students. If they show any wish to include the poem in classroom discussion and comparison with the Roman soldiers of "Today Is Friday" and Harold Krebs of „Soldier's Home" then this is all to the good. The key phrase, which links the three texts and may be useful in interpretation, is "I don't know why" (**26** 4).

2. After reading three Hemingway stories the students will now be familiar with many of the characteristics of Hemingway's style. The following parody of the Hemingway style by Robert Neumann can be used to round off Part III of the present course.

Flick

Nach Ernest Hemingway

Ich ging den Film sehn, Samstag. Ich nahm Flick mit ihn ansehn. Ich holte sie ab. Sie hatte schon was getrunken. Sie sah fein aus.

»Hullo, Blitz«, sagte sie. »What are you round for, this hour?«

»Film«, sagte ich.

»Willst du zuerst einen Whisky?«

»Sicher will ich.«

Ich goß mir einen Whisky ein und einen für Flick. Sie hatte schon ein paar gehabt. Sie nahm noch einen. Dann nahmen wir jeder noch zwei. Es war fein, dazusitzen und Flick anzusehen. Sie sah fein aus.

»Du siehst fein aus«, sagte ich.

»Fein«, sagte sie. »What are you round for, this hour?«

»Film.«

»Gut, gehn wir Film.«

Es war ein Film mit Präriepferden und Indianern. Ein scheues Pferd ging einen an, er wich aus und schlitzte ihm mit dem Messer den Bauch auf. Das Pferd traf ihn mit dem Huf vor die Brust, daß ihm das Brustbein eingedrückt worden wäre, wenn das nicht leider ein Film gewesen wäre, sondern wirklich. Aber er war ein feiner Kerl, er schmiß sich noch einmal vor mit dem Messer, er zielte noch einmal auf den Bauch, nun fielen dem Roß die Gedärme vor, und das war echt. Schade, daß sein Brustbein nicht echt war. Es war ein feiner Kampf. Ich mag Indianer gern und ich mag Pferde, es war fein, wie feine Kämpfer die zwei waren und einander zu Tode schindeten. Am Ende waren sie beide nur mehr Blut und Gedärme.

»Fein«, sagt ich.

»Gehen wir«, sagte Flick. »Ich mag die Gedärme nicht. Ich mag die beiden in der Großaufnahme nicht, sie schwitzen.«

»Fein«, sagte ich. »Gehen wir wohin, wo man Whisky kriegt.«

Als wir hinauskamen, regnete es.

»Regen«, sagte Flick.

»Gehn wir wohin, wo es Whisky gibt«, sagte ich.

»Fein. Der Film war fein, aber zuviel geschwitzt. Gehen wir Whisky.«

»Zu Fuß? Zu naß.«

»Naß, ja«, sagte Flick. »Es ist meistens naß, wenn es regnet.«

»Das Kaffeehaus drüben zu voll. Hast du noch Whisky zu Hause? Wir gehen zu dir.«

»Ja. Nein.«

»Ja – was?«

»Whisky zu Haus.«

»Und nein?«

»Nicht gehen. Zu naß. Auch der Kuß von den beiden im Film war zu naß.«

»Geschwitzt«, sagte ich.

»Zuviel«, sagte sie.

»Die Gedärme waren fein. Feine Kämpfer.«

»Gehen wir Whisky«, sagt sie.

»Zu Fuß?«

»Vielleicht trägt uns wer.«

Robert Neumann, *Die Parodien,* München o.J. (Kurt Desch), pp. 322–323.

PART IV

Bajonetten steken omgekeerd in het zand, ten teeken, dat hier een zwaargewonde is blijven liggen.

Bayonets stuck in the sand, showing that a heavily wounded soldier lies here.

Bajonette stecken verkehrt im Sand, zum Zeichen, dass hier ein Schwerverwundeter liegen geblieben ist.

Des baïonnettes, dressées de travers dans le sable, comme signe qu'à ce lieu un soldat gravement blessé a été abandonné.

A Vignette from *In Our Time*

While the bombardment was knocking the trench to pieces at Fossalta, he lay very flat and sweated and prayed oh jesus christ get me out of here. Dear jesus please get me out. Christ please please please christ. If you'll only keep me from getting killed I'll do anything you say. I believe in you and I'll tell everyone in the world that you are the only one that matters. Please please dear jesus. The shelling moved further up the line. We went to work on the trench and in the morning the sun came up and the day was hot and muggy and cheerful and quiet. The next night back at Mestre he did not tell the girl he went upstairs with at the Villa Rossa about Jesus. And he never told anybody.

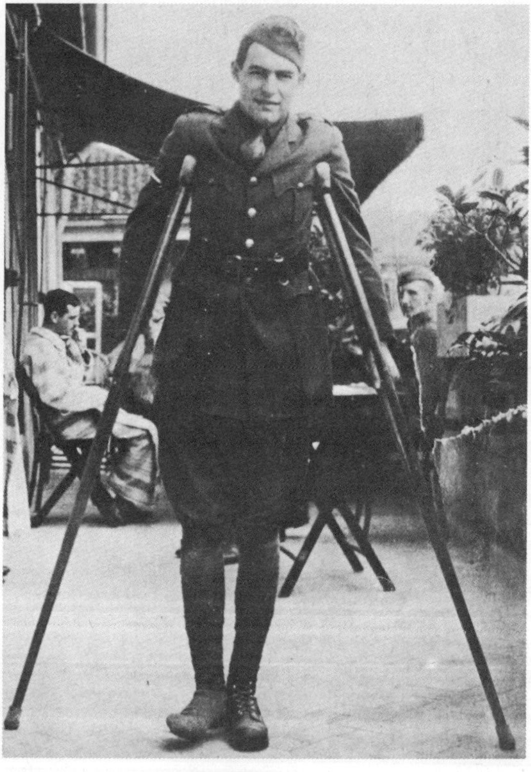

On July 8, 1918, Ernest Hemingway was severely wounded in a trench near Fossalta. The photograph shows him recovering on Lago Maggiore later that year.

A Way You'll Never Be

The attack had gone across the field, been held up by machine-gun fire from the sunken road and from the group of farm houses, encountered no resistance in the town, and reached the bank of the river. Coming along the road on a bicycle, getting off to push the machine when the surface of the road became too broken, Nicholas Adams saw what had happened by the position of the dead.

They lay alone or in clumps in the high grass of the field and along the road, their pockets out, and over them were flies and around each body or group of bodies were the scattered papers.

In the grass and the grain, beside the road, and in some places scattered over the road, there was much material: a field kitchen, it must have come over when things were going well; many of the calf-skin-covered haversacks, stick bombs, helmets, rifles, sometimes one butt-up, the bayonet stuck in the dirt, they had dug quite a little at the last; stick bombs, helmets, rifles, intrenching tools, ammunition boxes, star-shell pistols, their shells scattered about, medical kits, gas masks, empty gas-mask cans, a squat, tripodded machine gun in a nest of empty shells, full belts protruding from the boxes, the water-cooling can empty and on its side, the breech block gone, the crew in odd positions, and around them, in the grass, more of the typical papers.

There were mass prayer books, group postcards showing the machine-gun unit standing in ranked and ruddy cheerfulness as in a football picture for a college annual; now they were humped and swollen in the grass; propaganda postcards showing a soldier in Austrian uniform bending a woman backward over a bed; the figures were impressionistically drawn; very attractively depicted and had nothing in common with actual rape in which the woman's skirts are pulled over her head to smother her, one comrade sometimes sitting upon the head. There were many of these inciting cards which had evidently been issued just before the offensive. Now they were scattered with the smutty postcards, photographic; the small photographs of village girls by village photographers, the occasional pictures of children, and

9 **scattered** lying about everywhere – 16 **tripodded** [ˈtraɪpɒdɪd] resting on three legs – 22 **humped** lying in the shape of a round lump – 25 **rape** (Vergewaltigung) – 26 **to smother s.o.** [ˈsmʌðə] to prevent s.o. from breathing – 27 **to incite** to stir up – 29 **smutty** dirty

the letters, letters, letters. There was always much paper about the dead and the débris of this attack was no exception.

These were new dead and no one had bothered with anything but their pockets. Our own dead, or what he thought of, still, as our own dead, were surprisingly few, Nick noticed. Their coats had been opened too and their pockets were out, and they showed, by their positions, the manner and the skill of the attack. The hot weather had swollen them all alike regardless of nationality.

The town had evidently been defended, at the last, from the line of the sunken road and there had been few or no Austrians to fall back into it. There were only three bodies in the street and they looked to have been killed running. The houses of the town were broken by the shelling and the street had much rubble of plaster and mortar and there were broken beams, broken tiles, and many holes, some of them yellow-edged from the mustard gas. There were many pieces of shell, and shrapnel balls were scattered in the rubble. There was no one in the town at all.

Nick Adams had seen no one since he had left Fornaci, although, riding along the road through the over-foliaged country, he had seen guns hidden under screens of mulberry leaves to the left of the road, noticing them by the heat-waves in the air above the leaves where the sun hit the metal. Now he went on through the town, surprised to find it deserted, and came out on the low road beneath the bank of the river. Leaving the town there was a bare open space where the road slanted down and he could see the placid reach of the river and the low curve of the opposite bank and the whitened, sun-baked mud where the Austrians had dug. It was all very lush and over-green since he had seen it last and becoming historical had made no change in this, the lower river.

The battalion was along the bank to the left. There was a series of holes in the top of the bank with a few men in them. Nick noticed where the machine guns were posted and the signal rockets in their racks. The men in the holes in the side of the bank were sleeping. No one challenged. He went on and as he came around a turn in the mud bank a young second lieutenant with a stubble of beard and red-rimmed, very bloodshot eyes pointed a pistol at him.

"Who are you?"

Nick told him.

11 **they looked to have been killed** they looked as if they had been killed – 13 **rubble** stones, broken wood, etc. of destroyed houses – 15 **shell** a metal case filled with explosive and fired from a large gun – 23 **placid** [ˈplæsɪd] peaceful – 25 **lush** (üppig)

"How do I know this?"

Nick showed him the *tessera* with photograph and identification and the seal of the third army. He took hold of it.

"I will keep this."

"You will not," Nick said. "Give me back the card and put your gun away. There. In the holster."

"How am I to know who you are?"

"The *tessera* tells you."

"And if the *tessera* is false? Give me that card."

"Don't be a fool," Nick said cheerfully. "Take me to your company commander."

"I should send you to battalion headquarters."

"All right," said Nick. "Listen, do you know the Captain Paravicini? The tall one with the small mustache who was an architect and speaks English?"

"You know him?"

"A little."

"What company does he command?"

"The second."

"He is commanding the battalion."

"Good," said Nick. He was relieved to know that Para was all right. "Let us go to the battalion."

As Nick had left the edge of the town three shrapnel had burst high and to the right over one of the wrecked houses and since then there had been no shelling. But the face of this officer looked like the face of a man during a bombardment. There was the same tightness and the voice did not sound natural. His pistol made Nick nervous.

"Put it away," he said. "There's the whole river between them and you."

"If I thought you were a spy I would shoot you now," the second lieutenant said.

"Come on," said Nick. "Let us go to the battalion." This officer made him very nervous.

The Captain Paravicini, acting major, thinner and more English-looking than ever, rose when Nick saluted from behind the table in the dugout that was battalion headquarters.

"Hello," he said. "I didn't know you. What are you doing in that uniform?"

"They've put me in it."

"I am very glad to see you, Nicolo."

"Right. You look well. How was the show?"

"We made a very fine attack. Truly. A very fine attack. I will show you. Look."

He showed on the map how the attack had gone.

"I came from Fornaci," Nick said. "I could see how it had been. It was very good."

"It was extraordinary. Altogether extraordinary. Are you attached to the regiment?"

"No. I am supposed to move around and let them see the uniform."

"How odd."

"If they see one American uniform that is supposed to make them believe others are coming."

"But how will they know it is an American uniform?"

"You will tell them."

"Oh. Yes, I see. I will send a corporal with you to show you about and you will make a tour of the lines."

"Like a bloody politician," Nick said.

"You would be much more distinguished in civilian clothes. They are what is really distinguished."

"With a homburg hat," said Nick.

"Or with a very furry fedora."

"I'm supposed to have my pockets full of cigarettes and postal cards and such things," Nick said. "I should have a musette full of chocolate. These I should distribute with a kind word and a pat on the back. But there weren't any cigarettes and postcards and no chocolate. So they said to circulate around anyway."

"I'm sure your appearance will be very heartening to the troops."

"I wish you wouldn't," Nick said. "I feel badly enough about it as it is. In principle, I would have brought you a bottle of brandy."

"In principle," Para said and smiled, for the first time, showing yellowed teeth. "Such a beautiful expression. Would you like some Grappa?"

"No, thank you," Nick said.

"It hasn't any ether in it."

"I can taste that still," Nick remembered suddenly and completely.

"You know I never knew you were drunk until you started talking coming back in the *camions*."

"I was stinking in every attack," Nick said.

22 **musette (bag)** small bag for personal belongings of an army officer – 36 **stinking** *slang* very drunk

"I can't do it," Para said. "I took it in the first show, the very first show, and it only made me very upset and then frightfully thirsty."

"You don't need it."

"You're much braver in an attack than I am."

"No," Nick said. "I know how I am and I prefer to get stinking. I'm not ashamed of it."

"I've never seen you drunk."

"No?" said Nick. "Never? Not when we rode from Mestre to Portogrande that night and I wanted to go to sleep and used the bicycle for a blanket and pulled it up under my chin?"

"That wasn't in the lines."

"Let's not talk about how I am," Nick said. "It's a subject I know too much about to want to think about it any more."

"You might as well stay here a while," Paravicini said. "You can take a nap if you like. They didn't do much to this in the bombardment. It's too hot to go out yet."

"I suppose there is no hurry."

"How are you really?"

"I'm fine. I'm perfectly all right."

"No. I mean really."

"I'm all right. I can't sleep without a light of some sort. That's all I have now."

"I said it should have been trepanned. I'm no doctor but I know that."

"Well, they thought it was better to have it absorb, and that's what I got. What's the matter? I don't seem crazy to you, do I?"

"You seem in top-hole shape."

"It's a hell of a nuisance once they've had you certified as nutty," Nick said. "No one ever has any confidence in you again."

"I would take a nap, Nicolo," Paravicini said. "This isn't battalion headquarters as we used to know it. We're just waiting to be pulled out. You oughtn't to go out in the heat now – it's silly. Use that bunk."

"I might just lie down," Nick said.

Nick lay on the bunk. He was very disappointed that he felt this way and more disappointed, even, that it was so obvious to Captain Paravicini. This

8 **Mestre** small town just NW of Venice; the other places mentioned are on the river Piave, NE of Venice – 15 **nap** *colloquial* short period of sleep – 23 **to trepan** [-ˈ-] to cut the skull with a surgical instrument – 26 **top-hole** *dated slang* excellent – 27 **nutty** *slang* mad

was not as large a dugout as the one where that platoon of the class of 1899, just out at the front, got hysterics during the bombardment before the attack, and Para had had him walk them two at a time outside to show them nothing would happen, he wearing his own chin strap tight across his mouth to keep his lips quiet. Knowing they could not hold it when they took it. Knowing it was all a bloody balls – If he can't stop crying, break his nose to give him something else to think about. I'd shoot one but it's too late now. They'd all be worse. Break his nose. They've put it back to five-twenty. We've only got four minutes more. Break that other silly bugger's nose and kick his silly ass out of here. Do you think they'll go over? If they don't, shoot two and try to scoop the others out some way. Keep behind them, sergeant. It's no use to walk ahead and find there's nothing coming behind you. Bail them out as you go. What a bloody balls. All right. That's right. Then, looking at the watch, in that quiet tone, that valuable quiet tone, "Savoia." Making it cold, no time to get it, he couldn't find his own after the cave-in, one whole end had caved in; it was that started them; making it cold up that slope the only time he hadn't done it stinking. And after they came back the *teleferica* house burned, it seemed, and some of the wounded got down four days later and some did not get down, but we went up and we went back and we came down – we always came down. And there was Gaby Delys, oddly enough, with feathers on; you called me baby doll a year ago tadada you said that I was rather nice to know tadada with feathers on, with feathers off, the great Gaby, and my name's Harry Pilcer, too, we used to step out of the far side of the taxis when it got steep going up the hill and he could see that hill every night when he dreamed with Sacré Cœur, blown white, like a soap bubble. Sometimes his girl was there and sometimes she was with someone else and he could not understand that, but those were the nights the river ran so much wider and stiller than it should and outside of Fossalta there was a low house painted yellow with willows all around it and a low stable and there was a canal, and he had been there a thousand times and never seen it, but there it was every night as plain as the hill, only it frightened him. That house meant more than anything and every night he had it. That was what he needed but it frightened him especially when the

1 **the class of 1899** *here:* soldiers born in 1899 and drafted at the same time for military service – 6 **balls** *vulgar* mess, nonsense – 9 **bugger** *vulgar* fellow – 11 **to scoop out** *here:* to move out, i.e. to make the soldiers leave the dugout and start the attack – 13 **to bail out** cf. to scoop out – 15 **making it cold** succeeding in doing s.th. without being drunk – **to cave in** to collapse

boat lay there quietly in the willows on the canal, but the banks weren't like this river. It was all lower, as it was at Portogrande, where they had seen them come wallowing across the flooded ground holding the rifles high until they fell with them in the water. Who ordered that one? If it didn't get so damned mixed up he could follow it all right. That was why he noticed everything in such detail to keep it all straight so he would know just where he was, but suddenly it confused without reason as now, he lying in a bunk at battalion headquarters, with Para commanding a battalion and he in a bloody American uniform. He sat up and looked around; they all watching him. Para was gone out. He lay down again.

The Paris part came earlier and he was not frightened of it except when she had gone off with someone else and the fear that they might take the same driver twice. That was what frightened about that. Never about the front. He never dreamed about the front now any more but what frightened him so that he could not get rid of it was that long yellow house and the different width of the river. Now he was back here at the river, he had gone through that same town, and there was no house. Nor was the river that way. Then where did he go each night and what was the peril, and why would he wake, soaking wet, more frightened than he had ever been in a bombardment, because of a house and a long stable and a canal?

He sat up, swung his legs carefully down; they stiffened any time they were out straight for long; returned the stares of the adjutant, the signallers and the two runners by the door and put on his cloth-covered trench helmet.

"I regret the absence of the chocolate, the postal-cards and cigarettes," he said. "I am, however, wearing the uniform."

"The major is coming back at once," the adjutant said. In that army an adjutant is not a commissioned officer.

"The uniform is not very correct," Nick told them. "But it gives you the idea. There will be several millions of Americans here shortly."

"Do you think they will send Americans down here?" asked the adjutant.

"Oh, absolutely. Americans twice as large as myself, healthy, with clean hearts, sleep at night, never been wounded, never been blown up, never had their heads caved in, never been scared, don't drink, faithful to the girls they left behind them, many of them never had crabs, wonderful chaps. You'll see."

"Are you an Italian?" asked the adjutant.

3 **to wallow** ['wɒləʊ] to splash or roll about in – 18 **peril** danger

"No, American. Look at the uniform. Spagnolini made it but it's not quite correct."

"A North or South American?"

"North," said Nick. He felt it coming on now. He would quiet down.

"But you speak Italian."

"Why not? Do you mind if I speak Italian? Haven't I a right to speak Italian?"

"You have Italian medals."

"Just the ribbons and the papers. The medals come later. Or you give them to people to keep and the people go away; or they are lost with your baggage. You can purchase others in Milan. It is the papers that are of importance. You must not feel badly about them. You will have some yourself if you stay at the front long enough."

"I am a veteran of the Iritrea campaign," said the adjutant stiffly. "I fought in Tripoli."

"It's quite something to have met you," Nick put out his hand. "Those must have been trying days. I noticed the ribbons. Were you, by any chance, on the Carso?"

"I have just been called up for this war. My class was too old."

"At one time I was under the age limit," Nick said. "But now I am reformed out of the war."

"But why are you here now?"

"I am demonstrating the American uniform," Nick said. "Don't you think it is very significant? It is a little tight in the collar but soon you will see untold millions wearing this uniform swarming like locusts. The grasshopper, you know, what we call the grasshopper in America, is really a locust. The true grasshopper is small and green and comparatively feeble. You must not, however, make a confusion with the seven-year locust or cicada which emits a peculiar sustained sound which at the moment I cannot recall. I try to recall it but I cannot. I can almost hear it and then it is quite gone. You will pardon me if I break off our conversation?"

"See if you can find the major," the adjutant said to one of the two runners. "I can see you have been wounded," he said to Nick.

"In various places," Nick said. "If you are interested in scars I can show you some very interesting ones but I would rather talk about grasshoppers. What we call grasshoppers that is; and what are, really, locusts. These

17 **trying** extremely difficult or annoying – 18 **Carso** battlefield on the Italian-Yugoslav border – 25 **locust** ['ləʊkəst] (Wanderheuschrecke) – 28 **to emit** [ɪ'mɪt] to produce

insects at one time played a very important part in my life. It might interest you and you can look at the uniform while I am talking."

The adjutant made a motion with his hand to the second runner who went out.

"Fix your eyes on the uniform. Spagnolini made it, you know. You might as well look, too," Nick said to the signallers. "I really have no rank. We're under the American consul. It's perfectly all right for you to look. You can stare, if you like. I will tell you about the American locust. We always preferred one that we called the medium-brown. They last the best in the water and fish prefer them. The larger ones that fly making a noise somewhat similar to that produced by a rattlesnake rattling his rattlers, a very dry sound, have vivid colored wings, some are bright red, others yellow barred with black, but their wings go to pieces in the water and they make a very blowsy bait, while the medium-brown is a plump, compact, succulent hopper that I can recommend as far as one may well recommend something you gentlemen will probably never encounter. But I must insist that you will never gather a sufficient supply of these insects for a day's fishing by pursuing them with your hands or trying to hit them with a bat. That is sheer nonsense and a useless waste of time. I repeat, gentlemen, that you will get nowhere at it. The correct procedure, and one which should be taught all young officers at every small-arms course if I had anything to say about it, and who knows but what I will have, is the employment of a seine or net made of common mosquito netting. Two officers holding this length of netting at alternate ends, or let us say one at each end, stoop, hold the bottom extremity of the net in one hand and the top extremity in the other and run into the wind. The hoppers, flying with the wind, fly against the length of netting and are imprisoned in its folds. It is no trick at all to catch a very great quantity indeed, and no officer, in my opinion, should be without a length of mosquito netting suitable for the improvisation of one of these grasshopper seines. I hope I have made myself clear, gentlemen. Are there any questions? If there is anything in the course you do not understand please ask questions. Speak up. None? Then I would like to close on this note. In the words of that great soldier and gentleman, Sir Henry Wilson: Gentlemen, either you must govern or you must be governed. Let me repeat it. Gentlemen, there is one thing I would like to have you remember. One thing I would like you to take with you as you leave this room. Gentlemen, either you must govern – or you must be governed. That is all, gentlemen. Good-day."

13 **blowsy** *here:* lousy, i.e. no good at all – 22 **seine** [ˈseɪn] large fishing net

38

He removed his cloth-covered helmet, put it on again and, stooping, went out the low entrance of the dugout. Para, accompanied by the two runners, was coming down the line of the sunken road. It was very hot in the sun and Nick removed the helmet.

"There ought to be a system for wetting these things," he said. "I shall wet this one in the river." He started up the bank.

"Nicolo," Paravicini called. "Nicolo. Where are you going?"

"I don't really have to go." Nick came down the slope, holding the helmet in his hands. "They're a damned nuisance wet or dry. Do you wear yours all the time?"

"All the time," said Para. "It's making me bald. Come inside."

Inside Para told him to sit down.

"You know they're absolutely no damned good," Nick said. "I remember when they were a comfort when we first had them, but I've seen them full of brains too many times."

"Nicolo," Para said. "I think you should go back. I think it would be better if you didn't come up to the line until you had those supplies. There's nothing here for you to do. If you move around, even with something worth giving away, the men will group and that invites shelling. I won't have it."

"I know it's silly," Nick said. "It wasn't my idea. I heard the brigade was here so I thought I would see you or someone else I knew. I could have gone to Zenzon or to San Dona. I'd like to go to San Dona to see the bridge again."

"I won't have you circulating around to no purpose," Captain Paravicini said.

"All right," said Nick. He felt it coming on again.

"You understand?"

"Of course," said Nick. He was trying to hold it in.

"Anything of that sort should be done at night."

"Naturally," said Nick. He knew he could not stop it now.

"You see, I am commanding the battalion," Para said.

"And why shouldn't you be?" Nick said. Here it came. "You can read and write, can't you?"

"Yes," said Para gently.

"The trouble is you have a damned small battalion to command. As soon as it gets to strength again they'll give you back your company. Why don't they bury the dead? I've seen them now. I don't care about seeing them again. They can bury them any time as far as I'm concerned and it would be much better for you. You'll all get bloody sick."

"Where did you leave your bicycle?"

"Inside the last house."

"Do you think it will be all right?"

"Don't worry," Nick said. "I'll go in a little while."

"Lie down a little while, Nicolo."

"All right."

He shut his eyes, and in place of the man with the beard who looked at him over the sights of the rifle, quite calmly before squeezing off, the white flash and clublike impact, on his knees, hot-sweet choking, coughing it onto the rock while they went past him, he saw a long, yellow house with a low stable and the river much wider than it was and stiller. "Christ," he said, "I might as well go."

He stood up.

"I'm going, Para," he said. "I'll ride back now in the afternoon. If any supplies have come I'll bring them down tonight. If not I'll come at night when I have something to bring."

"It is still hot to ride," Captain Paravicini said.

"You don't need to worry," Nick said. "I'm all right now for quite a while. I had one then but it was easy. They're getting much better. I can tell when I'm going to have one because I talk so much."

"I'll send a runner with you."

"I'd rather you didn't. I know the way."

"You'll be back soon?"

"Absolutely."

"Let me send –"

"No," said Nick. "As a mark of confidence."

"Well, Ciaou then."

"Ciaou," said Nick. He started back along the sunken road toward where he had left the bicycle. In the afternoon the road would be shady once he had passed the canal. Beyond that there were trees on both sides that had not been shelled at all. It was on that stretch that, marching, they had once passed the Terza Savoia cavalry regiment riding in the snow with their lances. The horses' breath made plumes in the cold air. No, that was somewhere else. Where was that?

"I'd better get to that damned bicycle," Nick said to himself. "I don't want to lose the way to Fornaci."

Shell-shock

Shell-shock, a term for traumatic neurosis that was widely used during the First World War to describe various neurotic syndromes, which are now recognised as anxiety states and anxiety hysterias. Its invention and adoption may well have been facilitated by the preoccupation of the public mind at that time with the recently learned effects of high explosive. While it is true that the onset of symptoms was, in some cases, associated with some specific incident, such as proximity to a shell-burst, many more occurred in areas remote from shell-fire. The suggestion, seemingly implicit in such a term, that an important, or even essential, causal part was played by concussive trauma was as inaccurate as the picture which it tended to convey of a previously perfectly healthy individual being stricken down with dramatic suddenness. In the majority of cases the appearance of symptoms merely marked the point where the breaking stress had been reached after a prolonged period of tension, even if the latter had been unsuspected. The role played by any special incident was merely precipitant, and the true cause lay in conflict between the individual's instinct of self-preservation and the demands of patriotic duty, loyalty, and self-respect. The heavy emotional charge investing such a conflict finally became too strong, was dissociated from it, and erupted into consciousness as 'free' anxiety. The latter, or its somatic 'attachments,' accounted for a variety of signs and symptoms, such as tremor, inability to talk, paralysis, insomnia, amnesia, etc. These rendered the individual unfit for further service in the danger zone, revealing thereby their unconscious purposive aspect. Thus the original conflict had been solved in a manner involving no conscious guilt or loss of honour.

From *Everyman's Encyclopaedia*, Sixth Edition, London: J.M. Dent & Sons Ltd., 1978. Reprinted by permission.

Interpretation and Teaching Notes

Background

Hemingway's war experiences on the Italo-Austrian front in 1918 have already been described on p. 42. The campaign in which he played a decidedly minor but nonetheless heroic part has been described as perhaps the most senseless of the whole war.[1] From 1915 to 1918 about 680,000 Italians were killed. In the 11 battles on the Isonzo that were fought from May 1915 to October 1917 the Italian army managed to advance just 10 miles against the Austrians. It was a war of attrition, fought from trench to trench. In October 1917 an Austro-German counter-offensive drove the Italians back to the river Piave, only 25 miles north of Venice, in the battle of Caporetto. "Nearly 300,000 Italians were taken prisoner: even more deserted."[2] The British and French now sent considerable reinforcements to support the Italians, 11 divisions by the spring of 1918. In June 1918 a further Austrian attack took place but was repulsed by the Italians and their allies. It was this episode of the war that Hemingway was involved in, being wounded on July 8th. By July 17th he was in hospital in Milan, long before the decisive Italian counter-attack was launched in October 1918, a year after Caporetto. Austria capitulated on November 3rd 1918.[3] Hemingway's job in June–July 1918 had been to man one of the emergency canteens maintained by the American Red Cross in the small towns behind the Piave front. In this function Hemingway cheered up the Italian soldiers with supplies of "cigarettes, candy and postcards"[4] and perhaps his American uniform, with red enamel crosses on it, inspired the soldiers with a sense that there were allies ready at hand to support them.

---

1 Rudolf Lill, *Geschichte Italiens vom 16. Jahrhundert bis zu den Anfängen des Faschismus,* Darmstadt 1980, p. 276. Lill is the source for most of the information given here.

2 Alan Palmer, *The Penguin Dictionary of Twentieth Century History, 1900–1978,* Harmondsworth [3]1982, s.v. "Caporetto".

3 Lill comments: "Es ist jedoch festzuhalten, daß die eigentliche Leistung der italienischen Soldaten im Ersten Weltkrieg nicht der schließliche Sieg über 'die Reste eines der mächtigsten Heere', sondern das dreieinhalbjährige Durchhalten in einem überaus harten und verlustreichen Abnutzungs- und Stellungskrieg gewesen ist." (p. 287)

4 Baker 1969, p. 64.

Supplementary Texts

As so often in Hemingway, it is not the actual fighting and being wounded that is portrayed but rather a scene before or after action,[5] focussing on the mental and physical effects of warfare on the protagonist. It is noticeable that "A Way You'll Never Be" makes no mention of the reason for the fighting in general or of Nick's individual motivation. Baker quotes Hemingway as saying, in 1942: "I was an awful dope when I went to the last war. I can remember just thinking that we were the home team and the Austrians were the visiting team."[6] Reflections on the nature and meaning of war can thus only be made in terms of its effects. For this reason, Part IV of this reader contains two pictorial and two textual supplements to document such effects. The photograph on page 28, taken in September 1918 at Stresa, shows Hemingway on crutches, his right leg and foot still visibly swollen. The illustration on page 27 refers directly to the text of "A Way You'll Never Be" (**29** 13–14). As the caption explains, sticking a rifle bayonet down in the ground is a conventional sign "showing that a heavily [i.e. seriously] wounded soldier lies here", and would be understood in this sense by other soldiers or by ambulance men such as Hemingway.[7]

The article on "shell-shock" (**40**) has several functions. Hemingway could assume that his contemporary readers would be familiar with the concept, which does not itself occur in the story, and be able to identify Nick's behaviour as an instance of it. Young readers of today will not as a rule have such knowledge and so the text serves to bridge an information gap, making the story easier to understand without unduly suggesting any particular interpretation. Apart from providing information from a medical-psychological angle on the various causes of the battle neurosis that Nick demonstrates, it supplies some of the technical terms needed to discuss Nick's behaviour from that point on where the language of the story itself proves insufficient for analysis.

The second supplementary text (**28**) is the seventh vignette or interchapter from *In Our Time*. It renders the emotional impact of bombardment during trench warfare and thus is comparable both to the poem by Richard

5 Flora 1982, p. 108, makes this point and notes "The Killers" and "The Battler" as further examples.

6 Baker 1969, p. 57.

7 The picture and captions are from Ernst Friedrich, *Krieg dem Kriege!* (1924), p. 93, available as a cheap reprint from Zweitausendeins, 6000 Frankfurt 61, Postfach. Text and captions in this remarkable book are in four languages throughout.

Aldington (**21**) and to the depiction of anxiety and the need for comfort in faith found in “Today Is Friday”.

The supplements generally aim to help the students to discover individual approaches to “A Way You’ll Never Be”. If they are instructed to read the five texts of Part IV[8] with a view to what one contributes to an elucidation of the other, they will learn to propose questions of their own with less teacher guidance than would otherwise be necessary. That the ability to work out your own questions to a text is as important as the ability to answer someone else’s questions should be beyond dispute.[9]

Analysis

What is “A Way You’ll Never Be” about? Is it an indictment of war, of its brutality, destructiveness and senselessness? Or is it a study of fear and courage, exemplified in the experience of soldiers? Or the study of a nervous breakdown? Or is it a surrealist collage of states of consciousness, subconsciousness and dream? Or about true and false identities and about the true and false meaning of things and experiences?[10] All these approaches appear promising, and suitable questions and assignments are proposed on pages 98–100. There is something that all these themes have in common. They all raise the crucial question of how they can be expressed by language. How can one talk about war? How can one distinguish between fear and courage and with what words can one identify one’s own position with regard to them? How can one soldier tell another what the war has done to him and hope to be understood?

From the EFL point of view, this dominance of language as a theme can be put to good use in preparing the story for classroom discussion. The story contains a considerable amount of difficult vocabulary and a number of unfamiliar syntactical constructions. It also features snippets of French and Italian, Italian imitations of English and vice versa, technical vocabulary and some unexplained allusions to places and people. To have annotated all these would have meant swamping the text with so many definitions and explanations as to slow the students’ reading pace down practically to a halt.

8 Photographs, with or without explanatory captions, may be considered texts in the sense of being a system of signs which can be interpreted by an addressee.

9 Cf. *Richtlinien für die gymnasiale Oberstufe in Nordrhein-Westfalen: Englisch*, Köln 1981, pp. 87–88.

10 A good article is Geneviève Hily, “Langage et communication: un aspect inédit de la pensée de Hemingway,” *Etudes Anglaises* 22 (1969), pp. 279–292.

For this story, therefore (and the same applies to "The Short Happy Life of Francis Macomber") only as much annotation has been provided as the students on average will need for a first understanding of the gist of the story. It would be well to warn the students beforehand that they should not expect to understand everything – even the professional critics admit to being mystified.[11] They should be asked to concentrate on the sequence of events and not so much on the contents of the various dialogues or of Nick's interior monologue. At this stage a dictionary should *not* be used.

The sequence of events can be summarized thus:

A **29** 1 a) Nick, coming from Fornaci by bicycle, crosses a field over which the Italians have driven back the Austrians.
30 9 b) He comes to the town and passes through till he reaches the river bank where the Italian trenches are and sees the Austrian trenches on the opposite side.
B **30** 35 c) Nick encounters a young Italian second lieutenant who checks but doubts Nick's papers.
31 32 d) Nick is taken to Captain Paravicini whom he knows from earlier action.
C **33** 33 e) Nick lies down to rest. He reflects and remembers.
35 21 f) He gets up again, talks to the adjutant and starts to lecture him. The adjutant sends two soldiers off to get Paravicini.
D **38** 1 g) Nick and Paravicini talk.
39 27 h) Nick returns to Fornaci.

The divisions and subdivisions are only a rough guide. It is characteristic of this story that it resists cutting up into sections. There is rather a gradual movement from one "mode" to another. But what is this "mode"? In the first part of the story, as Nick is approaching the Italian trenches on the bank of the Piave, it is that of observing, identifying and interpreting. Nick, well trained in battle, recognizes all its various signs and knows what they mean. The prime example is the bayonets sticking in the sand, mentioned above, but there are numerous other signs of this kind. In fact there is a whole catalogue that adds up, more or less, to the concept of "battlefield". The second mode, in part B, is again one of identifying, but now it is a matter of self-identification. Nick has to prove to the Italian second lieutenant who he is, and in spite of the *tessera,* the identification, the Italian is not sure that Nick is not a spy, i.e. someone who pretends to be another. Captain Paravicini is of dubious identity in the same way – though Italian he

11 Young 1952, p. 25: "One never knows what is going on."

is "more English-looking than ever" (**31** 32–33), though a captain he is acting major. Paravicini does not recognize Nick because of his uniform, which turns out to be an Italian imitation of an American uniform by the Milanese tailor Spagnolini.[12] So Nick's appearance is false and his official task is to deceive: "I am supposed to move around and let them see the uniform. ... If they see one American uniform that is supposed to make them believe others are coming." (**32** 8–11) Then the two friends talk about past battles and bravery and it turns out that this military virtue was also a deception, being founded on nothing more than drunkenness. But at this point the issue of identity becomes more complex. Though Nick has impressed others as brave, he knows himself that he is not: "I know how I am" (**33** 5). Public identity is not the same as private identity. This poses a serious problem, one that is central to Hemingway's fiction: if the way I see myself is different from the way others see me, how can I hope for others ever to understand me? Nick is lucky in that Paravicini is extraordinarily understanding.

In part C, Nick rests on a bunk and lets his mind wander. Here the mode is remembering and associating. Names and events are associated in a way that defies temporal or causal logic and Nick can no longer interpret the divergent signs that come together in his mind: "If it didn't get so damned mixed up he could follow it all right" (**35** 4–5). Association remains the dominant mode in the following conversation between Nick and the adjutant. It is not a proper dialogue, of course, for where the adjutant is factual and literal, Nick is ironic and rambling. The Italian's way of making sense of things is different from the American's, so the one does not understand the other. Superficially, the reason for this is that Nick is undergoing a mental breakdown: "He felt it coming on now" (**36** 4), "it" being the neurosis described as shell-shock. Fundamentally, Nick is trying to come to terms with the experience of war, literally trying to find the terms or words that will allow him to master that experience. For it is a characteristic of language that it allows us to describe only those experiences which others have lived through and put into words before us and for us. Any new experience strains our ability to use language to the utmost. As we have seen in the stories previously dealt with in the course, this is Ernest Hemingway's enduring theme.

Nick's lecture on "The American locust, how to catch it, and its value as fishing bait" is the climax of the story. In its imitation of lecture-hall rhetoric, its pedantic precision and its absurd inappropriateness it is very

12 Baker 1969, p. 77.

funny. At the same time it is a poignant symptom and expression of Nick's mental state – an indictment of the war that has reduced him to this state.

The final part of the story describes the gradual return to normality and Nick's return to Fornaci. But things are still not what they seem to be, they have a special significance only accessible to someone with particular experience, a soldier for instance. They have a double identity. A helmet serves for protection, yet it has also been associated with death: "I've seen them full of brains too many times" (**38** 14–15). Nick does his best to distinguish between the present identity of things and their identity in his past experience, but it is not certain that he is able to do this. It is not even certain that he will manage *not* "to lose the way to Fornaci" (**39** 35). The final mode, then, would be that of making distinctions and trying to recover one's own identity. We are not told what Nick's success will be. As in all the stories we have dealt with up to now, there is an open ending.

An alternative way of presenting Nick's gradual descent into confusion as he suffers an attack of war neurosis is to plot it on a graph. This can only give a very rough picture but it does suggest how narrative tension is built up and relaxed again. It also shows how, with regard to geographical locations, Nick moves from reality to confusedly remembered past and back again.

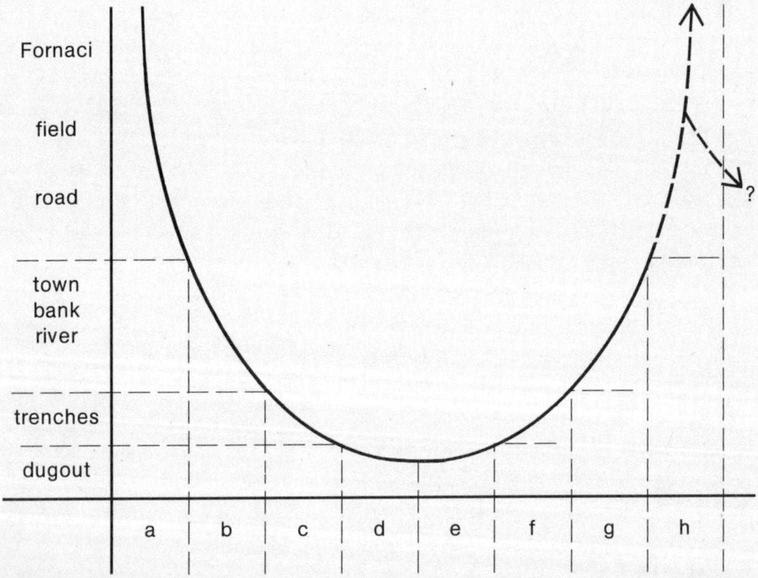

The column on the left shows how Nick moves towards neurosis the closer he gets to the river, for the closer he gets the more he confuses this section of the Piave with the one at Fossalta where he, like Hemingway, was wounded. Conversely, he seems to recover as soon as he can correctly identify his location, distinguishing this trench from the other dugout, "the one where that platoon of the class of 1899 ... got hysterics during the bombardment before the attack" (**34** 1–3). When he sets out for Fornaci again he is perhaps on the way to recovery, perhaps not.

First Unit: Action Past and Present

As a preparatory homework assignment the students should read the whole story, paying attention mainly to characters, places and the sequence of the action. As written work they should make a list of characters and places in order of mention and note the main events in their chronological sequence. This is an exercise in extensive or approximative reading (see above pp. 13–14). For this purpose the annotations at the foot of each page are sufficient, no additional vocabulary work being required at this stage.

1. *Briefly retell the present-time action of the story, i.e. excluding Nick's memories, in your own words.*
Nick, coming from Fornaci by bicycle, crosses a battlefield and reaches an unnamed town on the banks of a river (the Piave). He arrives at the trenches of an Italian battalion and is escorted by a second lieutenant to the acting commander, his old friend Captain Paravicini. They have a chat and Nick explains his current duties. Nick lies down to take a rest, then gets up again and lectures some Italian soldiers on the use of locusts as fishing-bait. Paravicini returns and sends Nick back to Fornaci.

2. *What are we told and what can we infer about the events prior to Nick's arrival at the trenches? See sections a) to d).*
a) As Nick crosses the battlefield he sees bodies and débris from which he can tell "what had happened" (**29** 5). The Italians have driven back the Austrians, killed many of them and robbed the dead bodies, strewing papers, letters and photographs all over the field. All kinds of weapons have been used, including gas. It was "a very fine attack", as Paravicini later says (**32** 1).
b) The town is quite empty, most houses have been destroyed and there are traces of the use of mustard gas. (Mustard gas, also known as Yellow Cross, is a powerful blister producer, and affects the eyes and respiratory tract after a period during which the effects are not obvious.) The Austrians have

retreated across the river and dug new trenches. The Italian soldiers are entrenched on the west bank of the Piave.
c) Nick holds an Italian military identity card *(tessera)* which shows him to be attached to the third army. Nick can see that the Italian second lieutenant is still suffering from the effects of an earlier bombardment, in other words Nick knows the symptoms when he sees them, undoubtedly from his own experience.
d) Nick knows Captain Paravicini – they have seen action together. Nick used to get drunk on Grappa mixed with ether before an attack. He seems to have suffered a head injury which perhaps has not been properly treated.

3. *What does Nick remember when he lies down?* (Section e)
During an unspecified earlier bombardment Nick, on Paravicini's orders, had to lead a platoon of inexperienced young soldiers out of the trenches into the open so as to get them used to the explosions and to prevent further hysterics – a sort of shock therapy. Nick gives a rather incoherent account of an uphill attack (due to begin at 5.20). During the attack a part of the covered trenches collapsed (**34** 15–16) and the station of the cable-railway evidently used for transporting the wounded was burned down. But we cannot be sure if this is really what happened – Nick is not a reliable narrator.

Next Nick thinks of some people he knew in Paris – Gaby Delys, Harry Pilcer (?) – before he arrived in Italy. He remembers the steep hill that leads to the Sacré Cœur church in Paris (a parallel to the "attack up that slope", **34** 16–17) and the fun they had cheating the taxi drivers out of their fares.

Then Nick remembers "that hill" (**34** 25) again, i.e. the slope up which the attack went, and the canal at Fossalta with the "low house painted yellow" (**34** 29), which in turn reminds him of the present river scene and another similar river scene at Portogrande. So he brings together in his memory the hills or slopes of Sacré Cœur, Fossalta, Portogrande and his present location.

The students' answers, which will of course only come bit by bit and as the result of some detective work, can be summarized in a blackboard sketch (see p. 97).

This is simply a way of sorting out Nick's memories, as far as his confused narrative permits us to. Paris is the location of pre-war experience, and both geographically and in the two remembered fears it prefigures the war. Fossalta, where Nick was wounded, is the central location of the war from the protagonist's point of view. Portogrande represents fear before the event and the present scene of our story the fear afterwards.

Paris	Portogrande	Fossalta	"here"
banks of the Seine?	low banks	banks of the canal	low banks of the Piave
Sacré Cœur hill (cable-car)	–	slope/hill cable-car *(teleferica)*	–
Seine?	water	canal	river
–	–	trenches/dugout	trenches/dugout
peace	war		
fear of unfaithfulness fear of taxi drivers	fear of death		

The teacher might like to confirm the results of the discussion and at the same time underline Hemingway's lifelong obsession with these events by giving the class a suitable passage from *Across the River and Into the Trees* (1950) to read (see *For Further Study* p. 101).

4. *Why does Nick try so hard to distinguish his various memories and why does he get them confused after all?*
This is another way of asking the question that Nick puts to himself (**35** 18–20). It refers to section e).

To be able to distinguish reality from memory and memory from nightmare is to be sane. Nick is trying hard to fend off another attack of "shell-shock". The reason "why he noticed everything in such detail" is that he wants "to keep it all straight" (**35** 5–6).

Nick tells himself that "that was what he needed" (**34** 33), i.e. the clear plain memory of what happened to him at Fossalta. The trouble is that this does not remain a neat, separate memory which he can firmly locate as "past" and so make it harmless. The traumatic events of the past invade both present experiences and memories of a more distant, happier time.

Second Unit: A Portrait of War

Fighting and killing, in one form or another, are perhaps Hemingway's most consistent themes. In this unit our aim is to describe with reference to "A Way You'll Never Be" what Hemingway's attitude to war is, or, from a different point of view, what the meaning of Nick's experience as a soldier can be for the reader. This theme has been touched upon in Part II, and more indirectly in Part III.

We begin with a simple alternative question and then try to follow up the different views proposed by the students.

1. *Is this an anti-war story, or is it a celebration of man's heroism in the face of war? Or what is your general impression?*
Brief reports of individual students' general impressions are called for here, not a detailed marshalling of the evidence.

2. *Collect all the information about the effects of war that are given in the story.*
This is an assignment for group work (or homework), with each group collecting the evidence for one or two specific effects and reporting its findings to the whole class. The teacher can suggest some of the subjects and ask for the students to suggest others. Some of the subjects and references are as follows:

Death	**29** 6, 13–14, 18–19, 22; **30** 3–8, 11–12; **38** 14–15, 36–39
Destruction	**29** 4–5; **30** 12–16
Indecency	**29** 23–29
Robbery	**30** 5–6
Fear	**31** 24–26; **33** 3–6; **34** 2–10, 27–33; **35** 11–20, 31–34
Madness	**33** 25–28, 33–34; **35** 7; **38** 26, 28–30, 32–33
Courage	**34** 4–5, 13–14; **35** 31–34; **36** 8–17

3. *Compare the effects of war described in this story with the rendering of the theme in Richard Aldington, "Bombardment", W. H. Auden, "Roman Wall Blues", "Soldier's Home" or the vignette no. 7 from* In Our Time.
This is again an assignment for group work or homework, i.e. always a comparison of just two texts. A general discussion can then take place in class. From the point of view of textual interpretation, the point of this exercise is to stress the fact that a complex and controversial subject like war is never exhausted in one text. Different texts "add up" to a composite picture, each contributing its partial version to the reader's understanding. The teacher can also point out and perhaps document with additional texts that the texts presented here all represent attitudes which are typical of the period after the first World War and that earlier or later texts will express significantly different ideas. The inability of any single text to provide a whole view is paralleled in and reflected by Nick Adams' inability to give a coherent report even of his own, authentic experience.

Third Unit: Make-believe or Truth?

"A Way You'll Never Be" features a number of instances of pretence or make-believe, in language as in behaviour. The most striking example is Nick dressed up in an imitation American uniform (**32** 8–14, **35** 25). Nick's official function is to be a morale booster, i.e. to make the Italians believe that he is the first of many American soldiers who will come to reinforce the Italian troops (**35** 28–31). This function is the same as that of the propaganda postcards Nick finds on the battlefield (**29** 22–28). The key word here is "supposed to" (**32** 8 and emphatically repeated 10 and 21). It is varied as "should" (**32** 22, 23) and "in principle" (**32** 27–29). This passage can be read and discussed in class and taken as a starting point for the following questions on the theme of make-believe in the story.

1. *What does Paravincini mean when he says, "Such a beautiful expression" (***32** *30)?*
The expression "in principle" (not to be confused with "on principle") is one that is used to justify or excuse an exception from the rule. But it is not the exception that things go wrong in a war, it is the rule. So Paravicini is being ironical, i.e. saying one thing while meaning the opposite. This is an everyday form of linguistic deception.

2. *Comment on the use of the following expressions:*
- "show" (**31** 39; **33** 1) – a euphemism for "attack"
- "You look well" (**31** 39; cf. **33** 18) – flattery, a "white lie"
- "You seem in top-hole shape" (**33** 26) – reassuring white lie
- "there will be several millions of Americans here shortly" (**35** 29; cf. **36** 23–25) – exaggeration (hyperbole as a satire on propaganda language)
- "Americans twice as large as myself" (**35** 31–35) – ironic hyperbole
- "it", "one", "they" (**36** 4; **38** 28 and 32; **39** 18–19) – euphemisms for "attack of shell-shock neurosis"

All these are examples of linguistic make-believe or lying. They all occur in direct speech or interior monologue, i.e. they express the speaker's reluctance to say the whole truth about something. An expression like "show" indicates that war is a taboo subject, that it is so horrible that it cannot be referred to directly or even that war is so immoral that it produces, inevitably, lies and evasions.

3. *How can the following be interpreted as make-believe? How do they contribute to the idea that war is deception?*
a) Nick in American uniform; b) getting drunk before battle; c) the symptoms

of shell-shock (cf. the definition **40** 30–40); d) *"I don't want to lose the way to Fornaci"* (**39** 34–35).

a) Nick's uniform is not a genuine American one, but a "not quite correct" (**36** 1–2 and **35** 28) copy by the Milan tailor Spagnolini. It is intended to give the Italians the false impression that strong American reinforcements are under way. It does not help the Italian adjutant to correctly identify Nick (**36** 3). The uniform thus serves to deceive and to disguise the inefficient canteen service (**35** 24–25). The uniform can be seen as a false clue, contrasting with the many clues which Nick sees and is able to interpret correctly as he crosses the battlefield.

b) Getting drunk is a form of self-deception, a way of hiding fear and pretending to be courageous.

c) Shell-shock is a psychological reaction which can be interpreted as a form of escape from "conscious guilt or loss of honour" (**40** 50–51).

d) The emphatic position of this statement at the end of the story suggests that it means rather more than it seems to say. Nick doesn't merely want to get safely back to Fornaci; he wants to reassure himself that by finding back to his base (like Harold trying to find back home) he can prove his sanity – to himself and to others.

Fourth Unit: A Way I'll Never Be?

What does the title of the story mean? Who is Hemingway addressing? What has Nick's experience got to do with me, the reader? Am I able to talk about the things I am afraid of? Is make-believe a feature of our daily lives? Can you give any examples? What are Nick's standards of behaviour, what are his motives? Can I understand or share them?

Any number of questions of this kind will arise in the course of the discussion of the story. It is suggested that the teacher should encourage his students to voice their own questions at this point in the course.[13] A good starting point for this is the title of the story. Philip Young comments on the title in a curious parenthesis: "'A Way You'll Never Be' (one depends on

13 The importance of the reader putting himself in the place of a fictional character is described by Lothar Bredella, "Die Struktur der Interaktion und das Verstehen literarischer Texte im Unterricht", *Der fremdsprachliche Unterricht* 13 (1979), pp. 37–50.

it)."[14] But can one really depend on it? Surely the "promise" that Nick's experience can never be ours is a wholly irresponsible one. It would turn Nick into a clinical case of neurosis, of interest only to a psychologist. It makes more sense to read the title as ironical, perhaps even as a warning that we may have to share Nick's experience.

No attempt is made here to propose a set of questions, still less of answers – these should arise out of the unpredictable situation in each individual class.

For Further Study

1. The German translation of this story by Annemarie Horschitz-Horst could be compared with the original. Two or three good students should be able to detect the numerous mistakes, inaccuracies and instances of unidiomatic German in the translation. It would be sufficient to compare one of those passages which are enigmatic in the original, e.g. section e).[15]

2. An interesting extension, which shows up links between "Soldier's Home", "The End of Something" and "A Way You'll Never Be", is to read "Big Two-Hearted River".

3. As suggested above, a brief passage from *Across the River and Into the Trees* can be presented in class as a document of how Hemingway interpreted the fighting on the Piave much later in life, through the eyes of the fictional character Colonel Cantwell.

> The Austrian attacks were ill-co-ordinated, but they were constant and exasperated and you first had the heavy bombardment which was supposed to put you out of business, and then, when it lifted, you checked your positions and counted the people. But you had no time to care for the wounded, since you knew that the attack was coming immediately, and then you killed the men who came wading across the marshes, holding their rifles above the water and coming as slow as men wade, waist deep.
>
> If they did not lift the shelling when it started, the Colonel, then a lieutenant, often thought, I do not know what we would be able to do. But they always lifted it and moved it back ahead of the attack.
>
> If we had lost the old Piave and were on the Sile they would move it back to the second and third lines; although such lines were quite untenable, and they should have brought all their guns up very close and whammed it in all the time

14 Young 1952, p. 23.

15 Ernest Hemingway, *Die Nick Adams Stories,* Hamburg 1973, rororo 5091 "So, wie du niemals sein wirst", pp. 150–164.

they attacked and until they breached us. But thank God, some high fool always controls it, the Colonel thought, and they did it piecemeal.

All that winter, with a bad sore throat, he had killed men who came, wearing the stick bombs hooked up on a harness under their shoulders with the heavy, calf-hide packs and the bucket helmets. They were the enemy.

But he never hated them; nor could have any feeling about them. He commanded with an old sock around his throat, which had been dipped in turpentine, and they broke down the attacks with rifle fire and with the machine guns which still existed, or were usable, after the bombardment. He taught his people to shoot, really, which is a rare ability in continental troops, and to be able to look at the enemy when they came, and, because there was always a dead moment when the shooting was free, they became very good at it.

But you always had to count and count fast after the bombardment to know how many shooters you would have. He was hit three times that winter, but they were all gift wounds; small wounds in the flesh of the body without breaking bone, and he had become quite confident of his personal immortality since he knew he should have been killed in the heavy artillery bombardment that always preceded the attacks. Finally, he did get hit properly and for good. No one of his other wounds had ever done to him what the first big one did. I suppose it is just the loss of the immortality, he thought. Well, in a way, that is quite a lot to lose.

Across the River and Into the Trees, New York: Charles Scribner's Sons, 1950, pp. 32–33.

4. An alternative text, which can be used to help understand "A Way You'll Never Be", is from Malcolm Cowley's recollections of Hemingway. About the wounding at Fossalta Cowley reports:

"There was one of those big noises you sometimes hear at the front," Ernest told a friend much later. "I died then. I felt my soul or something coming right out of my body like you'd pull a silk handkerchief out of a pocket by one corner. It flew all around and then came back and went in again and I wasn't dead any more." [...]

"In the first war I was hurt very badly; in the body, mind, and spirit and also morally," he told me thirty years later. "The true gen* is I was hurt bad all the way through and I was truly spooked in the end." Perhaps that was the origin of a contrast between the public and the private Hemingway that was to persist all through his life. Publicly he was a war hero and a real one, too, considering the courage and instinctive presence of mind he had shown in an emergency. [...] Privately, though, be was and for a long time would remain a frightened man.

---

* **gen** *British slang* general information; *here:* **the true gen** the truth

Malcolm Cowley, *A Second Flowering: Works and Days of the Lost Generation,* London 1973, pp. 224–225.

Additional Vocabulary

As explained on pp. 13 and 14, the amount of vocabulary annotation in the pupil's book has been kept to a minimum. In the case of the two longer stories, "A Way You'll Never Be" and "The Short Happy Life of Francis Macomber," this course has been adopted in order to encourage extensive reading as a first step. When individual sections of these stories are set for classroom discussion, etc. the teacher can choose between several kinds of vocabulary work. He can have his students practise dictionary work with a suitable English learner's dictionary or he can provide them with vocabulary worksheets. The latter can be given as a complete supplementary list, as below, or in the form of a thematic lexical field, e.g. on slang or on military vocabulary. The following list contains those items of vocabulary not explained in the pupil's book.

29 2 **to encounter** to meet with – 12 **haversack** ['hævəsæk] bag carried on the back, esp. as used by soldiers – 13 **stick bomb** handgrenade with a stick to hold it by – 15 **intrenching tools** spades, etc. needed to dig trenches – **star shell** shell (grenade) designed to burst high in the air and light up the enemy position – 16 **kit** set of equipment – **squat** [skwɒt] short and thick – 17 **to protrude** to stick out – 18 **breech block** movable piece of metal in a gun – 21 **ranked** standing according to military rank – **ruddy** having a healthy reddish colour (of the cheeks) – 22 **swollen** ['swəʊlən]

30 2 **débris** ['deɪbri:] scattered broken pieces – 13 **plaster** (Gips) – **mortar** (Mörtel) – **beam** long piece of wood as used in building roofs – 14 **tile** thin slab of baked clay used to cover a roof – 18 **foliage** ['fəʊlɪɪdʒ] leaves; **over-foliaged** is a synonym of over-green (25) – 19 **mulberry** (Maulbeere) – 23 **placid** ['plæsɪd] peaceful – **reach** *here:* section – 28 **battalion** [bə'tæljən]

31 2 **tessera** *Italian:* identity card – 6 **holster** leather pocket for a gun – 32 **acting** *here:* in the temporary function of

32 19 **homburg hat** soft felt hat – 20 **fedora** [fɪ'dɔ:rə] soft felt hat with curled brim – 30 **Grappa** kind of Italian brandy – 32 **ether** ['i:θə] (Äther) – 35 **camion** *Italian:* lorry

33 8 **Mestre** small town just NW of Venice – **Portogrande** Porto Grande, town on the Adriatic coast

34 14 **Savoia** the Terza Savoia (Third Savoyan) Cavalry Regiment, see **39** 31 – 18 **teleferica** [– –'– – –] *Italian:* cable railway – 20 **Gaby Delys** or **Deslys** Gaby was the name of a blonde French girl aboard the boat which brought Hemingway to Europe in 1918; the name is paradoxically ambiguous a) *des lys* of the lilies, suggesting purity, or b) *délice* pleasure, delight – 29 **Fossalta (di Piave)** village on the Piave, NE of Venice

35 1 **willow** (Weide) – 34 **crabs** *here:* crab lice (Filzläuse)

36 1 **Spagnolini** military tailor in Milan – 9 **ribbon** strip of silk representing a military decoration – 14 **Iritrea** Eritrea, province of Ethiopia, Italian colony from 1889 to 1941 – 28 **cicada** [sɪ'kɑ:də] (Baumgrille) – 29 **to sustain** [sə'steɪn] to keep up, to continue

37 12 **vivid** bright – **barred** striped – 14 **succulent** ['sʌkjʊlənt] juicy – 18 **sheer** *empha-*

tic complete, pure – 22 **who knows but what** perhaps – 24 **to stoop** to bend down – 26 **hoppers** *short for:* grasshoppers – 33 **Sir Henry Wilson** British general (1864–1922), well known as a public speaker

38 22 **Zenzon** Zenson di Piave, town south of Fossalta – **San Dona** town on the main road crossing the Piave, south of Zenson

39 7 **to squeeze off** to pull the trigger of a gun – 8 **club** (Keule) – 32 **plume** *here:* feathery cloud

PART V

Hemingway and his buffalo, Serengeti Plain, January 1934.

The Short Happy Life of Francis Macomber

It was now lunch time and they were all sitting under the double green fly of the dining tent pretending that nothing had happened.

"Will you have lime juice or lemon squash?" Macomber asked.

"I'll have a gimlet," Robert Wilson told him.

"I'll have a gimlet too. I need something," Macomber's wife said.

"I suppose it's the thing to do," Macomber agreed. "Tell him to make three gimlets."

The mess boy had started them already, lifting the bottles out of the canvas cooling bags that sweated wet in the wind that blew through the trees that shaded the tents.

"What had I ought to give them?" Macomber asked.

"A quid would be plenty," Wilson told him. "You don't want to spoil them."

4 **gimlet** [ˈgɪmlɪt] name of a cocktail – 6 **it's the thing to do** it is what one usually does in a case like this – 12 **quid** *slang* pound

"Will the headman distribute it?"

"Absolutely."

Francis Macomber had, half an hour before, been carried to his tent from the edge of the camp in triumph on the arms and shoulders of the cook, the personal boys, the skinner and the porters. The gun-bearers had taken no part in the demonstration. When the native boys put him down at the door of his tent, he had shaken all their hands, received their congratulations, and then gone into the tent and sat on the bed until his wife came in. She did not speak to him when she came in and he left the tent at once to wash his face and hands in the portable wash basin outside and go over to the dining tent to sit in a comfortable canvas chair in the breeze and the shade.

"You've got your lion," Robert Wilson said to him, "and a damned fine one too."

Mrs. Macomber looked at Wilson quickly. She was an extremely handsome and well-kept woman of the beauty and social position which had, five years before, commanded five thousand dollars as the price of endorsing, with photographs, a beauty product which she had never used. She had been married to Francis Macomber for eleven years.

"He is a good lion, isn't he?" Macomber said. His wife looked at him now. She looked at both these men as though she had never seen them before.

One, Wilson, the white hunter, she knew she had never truly seen before. He was about middle height with sandy hair, a stubby mustache, a very red face and extremely cold blue eyes with faint white wrinkles at the corners that grooved merrily when he smiled. He smiled at her now and she looked away from his face at the way his shoulders sloped in the loose tunic he wore with the four big cartridges held in loops where the left breast pocket should have been, at his big brown hands, his old slacks, his very dirty boots and back to his red face again. She noticed where the baked red of his face stopped in a white line that marked the circle left by his Stetson hat that hung now from one of the pegs of the tent pole.

"Well, here's to the lion," Robert Wilson said. He smiled at her again and, not smiling, she looked curiously at her husband.

Francis Macomber was very tall, very well built if you did not mind that length of bone, dark, his hair cropped like an oarsman, rather thin-lipped, and was considered handsome. He was dressed in the same sort of safari clothes that Wilson wore except that his were new, he was thirty-five years

16 **to command** to deserve and get, to fetch – **to endorse** [ɪnˈdɔːs] to give support to – 27 **cartridge** [ˈkɑːtrɪdʒ] (Patrone)

old, kept himself very fit, was good at court games, had a number of big-game fishing records, and had just shown himself, very publicly, to be a coward.

"Here's to the lion," he said. "I can't ever thank you for what you did."

Margaret, his wife, looked away from him and back to Wilson.

"Let's not talk about the lion," she said.

Wilson looked over at her without smiling and now she smiled at him.

"It's been a very strange day," she said. "Hadn't you ought to put your hat on even under the canvas at noon? You told me that, you know."

"Might put it on," said Wilson.

"You know you have a very red face, Mr. Wilson," she told him and smiled again.

"Drink," said Wilson.

"I don't think so," she said. "Francis drinks a great deal, but his face is never red."

"It's red today," Macomber tried a joke.

"No," said Margaret. "It's mine that's red today. But Mr. Wilson's is always red."

"Must be racial," said Wilson. "I say, you wouldn't like to drop my beauty as a topic, would you?"

"I've just started on it."

"Let's chuck it," said Wilson.

"Conversation is going to be so difficult," Margaret said.

"Don't be silly, Margot," her husband said.

"No difficulty," Wilson said. "Got a damn fine lion."

Margot looked at them both and they both saw that she was going to cry. Wilson had seen it coming for a long time and he dreaded it. Macomber was past dreading it.

"I wish it hadn't happened. Oh, I wish it hadn't happened," she said and started for her tent. She made no noise of crying but they could see that her shoulders were shaking under the rose-colored, sun-proofed shirt she wore.

"Women upset," said Wilson to the tall man. "Amounts to nothing. Strain on the nerves and one thing'n another."

"No," said Macomber. "I suppose that I rate that for the rest of my life now."

22 **to chuck s.th.** *BE slang* to throw s.th away, *here:* to give s.th. up – 27 **to dread** [dred] to be very much afraid of – 34 **to rate** to be regarded in a certain way – **I rate that ...** I will be considered that ...

"Nonsense. Let's have a spot of the giant killer," said Wilson. "Forget the whole thing. Nothing to it anyway."

"We might try," said Macomber. "I won't forget what you did for me though."

"Nothing," said Wilson. "All nonsense."

So they sat there in the shade where the camp was pitched under some wide-topped acacia trees with a boulder-strewn cliff behind them, and a stretch of grass that ran to the bank of a boulder-filled stream in front with forest beyond it, and drank their just-cool lime drinks and avoided one another's eyes while the boys set the table for lunch. Wilson could tell that the boys all knew about it now and when he saw Macomber's personal boy looking curiously at his master while he was putting dishes on the table he snapped at him in Swahili. The boy turned away with his face blank.

"What were you telling him?" Macomber asked.

"Nothing. Told him to look alive or I'd see he got about fifteen of the best."

"What's that? Lashes?"

"It's quite illegal," Wilson said. "You're supposed to fine them."

"Do you still have them whipped?"

"Oh, yes. They could raise a row if they chose to complain. But they don't. They prefer it to the fines."

"How strange!" said Macomber.

"Not strange, really," Wilson said. "Which would you rather do? Take a good birching or lose your pay?"

Then he felt embarrassed at asking it and before Macomber could answer he went on, "We all take a beating every day, you know, one way or another."

This was no better. "Good God," he thought. "I am a diplomat, aren't I?"

"Yes, we take a beating," said Macomber, still not looking at him. "I'm awfully sorry about that lion business. It doesn't have to go any further, does it? I mean no one will hear about it, will they?"

"You mean will I tell it at the Mathaiga Club?" Wilson looked at him now coldly. He had not expected this. So he's a bloody four-letter man as well as a bloody coward, he thought. I rather liked him too until today. But how is one to know about an American?

1 **giant killer** *here:* strong alcoholic drink – 15 **fifteen of the best** 15 strokes with a whip – 24 **birching** whipping, as with the branches of a birch tree – 33 **four-letter man** a man who can only be described by using an obscene or four-letter word

"No," said Wilson. "I'm a professional hunter. We never talk about our clients. You can be quite easy on that. It's supposed to be bad form to ask us not to talk though."

He had decided now that to break would be much easier. He would eat, then, by himself and could read a book with his meals. They would eat by themselves. He would see them through the safari on a very formal basis – what was it the French called it? Distinguished consideration – and it would be a damn sight easier than having to go through this emotional trash. He'd insult him and make a good clean break. Then he could read a book with his meals and he'd still be drinking their whisky. That was the phrase for it when a safari went bad. You ran into another white hunter and you asked, "How is everything going?" and he answered, "Oh, I'm still drinking their whisky," and you knew everything had gone to pot.

"I'm sorry," Macomber said and looked at him with his American face that would stay adolescent until it became middle-aged, and Wilson noted his crew-cropped hair, fine eyes only faintly shifty, good nose, thin lips and handsome jaw. "I'm sorry I didn't realize that. There are lots of things I don't know."

So what could he do, Wilson thought. He was all ready to break it off quickly and neatly and here the beggar was apologizing after he had just insulted him. He made one more attempt. "Don't worry about me talking," he said. "I have a living to make. You know in Africa no woman ever misses her lion and no white man ever bolts."

"I bolted like a rabbit," Macomber said.

Now what in hell were you going to do about a man who talked like that, Wilson wondered.

Wilson looked at Macomber with his flat, blue, machine-gunner's eyes and the other smiled back at him. He had a pleasant smile if you did not notice how his eyes showed when he was hurt.

"Maybe I can fix it up on buffalo," he said. "We're after them next, aren't we?"

"In the morning if you like," Wilson told him. Perhaps he had been wrong. This was certainly the way to take it. You most certainly could not tell a damned thing about an American. He was all for Macomber again. If you could forget the morning. But, of course, you couldn't. The morning had been about as bad as they come.

6 **to see s.o. through s.th.** to guide s.o. – 8 **trash** rubbish – 13 **to go to pot** to turn bad – 16 **shifty** not looking steadily in one direction – 23 **to bolt** to run away – 30 **to fix it up** to make up for it

"Here comes the Memsahib," he said. She was walking over from her tent looking refreshed and cheerful and quite lovely. She had a very perfect oval face, so perfect that you expected her to be stupid. But she wasn't stupid, Wilson thought, no, not stupid.

"How is the beautiful red-faced Mr. Wilson? Are you feeling better, Francis, my pearl?"

"Oh, much," said Macomber.

"I've dropped the whole thing," she said, sitting down at the table. "What importance is there to whether Francis is any good at killing lions? That's not his trade. That's Mr. Wilson's trade. Mr. Wilson is really very impressive killing anything. You do kill anything, don't you?"

"Oh, anything," said Wilson. "Simply anything." They are, he thought, the hardest in the world; the hardest, the cruelest, the most predatory and the most attractive and their men have softened or gone to pieces nervously as they have hardened. Or is it that they pick men they can handle? They can't know that much at the age they marry, he thought. He was grateful that he had gone through his education on American women before now because this was a very attractive one.

"We're going after buff in the morning," he told her.

"I'm coming," she said.

"No, you're not."

"Oh, yes, I am. Mayn't I, Francis?"

"Why not stay in camp?"

"Not for anything," she said. "I wouldn't miss something like today for anything."

When she left, Wilson was thinking, when she went off to cry, she seemed a hell of a fine woman. She seemed to understand, to realize, to be hurt for him and for herself and to know how things really stood. She is away for twenty minutes and now she is back, simply enamelled in that American female cruelty. They are the damnedest women. Really the damnedest.

"We'll put on another show for you tomorrow," Francis Macomber said.

"You're not coming," Wilson said.

"You're very mistaken," she told him. "And I want *so* to see you perform again. You were lovely this morning. That is if blowing things' heads off is lovely."

"Here's the lunch," said Wilson. "You're very merry, aren't you?"

"Why not? I didn't come out here to be dull."

13 **predatory** [ˈpredətərɪ] preying upon others, robbing, hunting

"Well, it hasn't been dull," Wilson said. He could see the boulders in the river and the high bank beyond with the trees and he remembered the morning.

"Oh, no," she said. "It's been charming. And tomorrow. You don't know how I look forward to tomorrow."

"That's eland he's offering you," Wilson said.

"They're the big cowy things that jump like hares, aren't they?"

"I suppose that describes them," Wilson said.

"It's very good meat," Macomber said.

"Did you shoot it, Francis?" she asked.

"Yes."

"They're not dangerous, are they?"

"Only if they fall on you." Wilson told her.

"I'm so glad."

"Why not let up on the bitchery just a little, Margot," Macomber said, cutting the eland steak and putting some mashed potato, gravy and carrot on the down-turned fork that tined through the piece of meat.

"I suppose I could," she said, "since you put it so prettily."

"Tonight we'll have champagne for the lion," Wilson said. "It's a bit too hot at noon."

"Oh, the lion," Margot said. "I'd forgotten the lion!"

So, Robert Wilson thought to himself, she *is* giving him a ride, isn't she? Or do you suppose that's her idea of putting up a good show? How should a woman act when she discovers her husband is a bloody coward? She's damn cruel but they're all cruel. They govern, of course, and to govern one has to be cruel sometimes. Still, I've seen enough of their damn terrorism.

"Have some more eland," he said to her politely.

That afternoon, late, Wilson and Macomber went out in the motor car with the native driver and the two gun-bearers. Mrs. Macomber stayed in the camp. It was too hot to go out, she said, and she was going with them in the early morning. As they drove off Wilson saw her standing under the big tree, looking pretty rather than beautiful in her faintly rosy khaki, her dark hair drawn back off her forehead and gathered in a knot low on her neck, her face as fresh, he thought, as though she were in England. She waved to them as the car went off through the swale of high grass and curved around through the trees into the small hills of orchard bush.

15 **to let up on** to go easy on, to reduce – **bitchery** aggressive behaviour, especially of women – 22 **to give s.o. a ride** to make fun of s.o., to humiliate s.o.

In the orchard bush they found a herd of impala, and leaving the car they stalked one old ram with long, wide-spread horns and Macomber killed it with a very creditable shot that knocked the buck down at a good two hundred yards and sent the herd off bounding wildly and leaping over one another's backs in long, leg-drawn-up leaps as unbelievable and as floating as those one makes sometimes in dreams.

"That was a good shot," Wilson said. "They're a small target."

"Is it a worth-while head?" Macomber asked.

"It's excellent," Wilson told him. "You shoot like that and you'll have no trouble."

"Do you think we'll find buffalo tomorrow?"

"There's a good chance of it. They feed out early in the morning and with luck we may catch them in the open."

"I'd like to clear away that lion business," Macomber said. "It's not very pleasant to have your wife see you do something like that."

I should think it would be even more unpleasant to do it, Wilson thought, wife or no wife, or to talk about it having done it. But he said, "I wouldn't think about that any more. Anyone could be upset by his first lion. That's all over."

But that night after dinner and a whisky and soda by the fire before going to bed, as Francis Macomber lay on his cot with the mosquito bar over him and listened to the night noises it was not all over. It was neither all over nor was it beginning. It was there exactly as it happened with some parts of it indelibly emphasized and he was miserably ashamed at it. But more than shame he felt cold, hollow fear in him. The fear was still there like a cold slimy hollow in all the emptiness where once his confidence had been and it made him feel sick. It was still there with him now.

It had started the night before when he had wakened and heard the lion roaring somewhere up along the river. It was a deep sound and at the end there were sort of coughing grunts that made him seem just outside the tent, and when Francis Macomber woke in the night to hear it he was afraid. He could hear his wife breathing quietly, asleep. There was no one to tell he was afraid, nor to be afraid with him, and, lying alone, he did not know the Somali proverb that says a brave man is always frightened three times by a lion; when he first sees his track, when he first hears him roar and when he first confronts him. Then while they were eating breakfast by lantern light

2 **to stalk** [stɔ:k] to approach carefully without being seen or heard – 24 **indelible** [ɪnˈdelɪbəl] which cannot be made to disappear

out in the dining tent, before the sun was up, the lion roared again and Francis thought he was just at the edge of camp.

"Sounds like an old-timer," Robert Wilson said, looking up from his kippers and coffee. "Listen to him cough."

"Is he very close?"

"A mile or so up the stream."

"Will we see him?"

"We'll have a look."

"Does his roaring carry that far? It sounds as though he were right in camp."

"Carries a hell of a long way," said Robert Wilson. "It's strange the way it carries. Hope he's a shootable cat. The boys said there was a very big one about here."

"If I get a shot, where should I hit him," Macomber asked, "to stop him?"

"In the shoulders," Wilson said. "In the neck if you can make it. Shoot for bone. Break him down."

"I hope I can place it properly," Macomber said.

"You shoot very well," Wilson told him. "Take your time. Make sure of him. The first one in is the one that counts."

"What range will it be?"

"Can't tell. Lion has something to say about that. Won't shoot unless it's close enough so you can make sure."

"At under a hundred yards?" Macomber asked.

Wilson looked at him quickly.

"Hundred's about right. Might have to take him a bit under. Shouldn't chance a shot at much over that. A hundred's a decent range. You can hit him wherever you want at that. Here comes the Memsahib."

"Good morning," she said. "Are we going after that lion?"

"As soon as you deal with your breakfast," Wilson said. "How are you feeling?"

"Marvellous," she said. "I'm very excited."

"I'll just go and see that everything is ready," Wilson went off. As he left the lion roared again.

"Noisy beggar," Wilson said. "We'll put a stop to that."

"What's the matter, Francis?" his wife asked him.

"Nothing," Macomber said.

3 **kipper** smoked herring

"Yes, there is," she said. "What are you upset about?"

"Nothing," he said.

"Tell me," she looked at him. "Don't you feel well?"

"It's that damned roaring," he said. "It's been going on all night, you know."

"Why didn't you wake me," she said. "I'd love to have heard it."

"I've got to kill the damned thing," Macomber said, miserably.

"Well, that's what you're out here for, isn't it?"

"Yes. But I'm nervous. Hearing the thing roar gets on my nerves."

"Well then, as Wilson said, kill him and stop his roaring."

"Yes, darling," said Francis Macomber. "It sounds easy, doesn't it?"

"You're not afraid, are you?"

"Of course not. But I'm nervous from hearing him roar all night."

"You'll kill him marvellously," she said. "I know you will. I'm awfully anxious to see it."

"Finish your breakfast and we'll be starting."

"It's not light yet," she said. "This is a ridiculous hour."

Just then the lion roared in a deep-chested moaning, suddenly guttural, ascending vibration that seemed to shake the air and ended in a sigh and a heavy, deep-chested grunt.

"He sounds almost here," Macomber's wife said.

"My God," said Macomber. "I hate that damned noise."

"It's very impressive."

"Impressive. It's frightful."

Robert Wilson came up then carrying his short, ugly, shockingly big-bored .505 Gibbs and grinning.

"Come on," he said. "Your gun-bearer has your Springfield and the big gun. Everything's in the car. Have you solids?"

"Yes."

"I'm ready," Mrs. Macomber said.

"Must make him stop that racket," Wilson said. "You get in front. The Memsahib can sit back here with me."

They climbed into the motor car and, in the gray first daylight, moved off up the river through the trees. Macomber opened the breech of his rifle and saw he had metal-cased bullets, shut the bolt and put the rifle on safety. He saw his hand was trembling. He felt in his pocket for more cartridges and moved his fingers over the cartridges in the loops of his tunic front. He turned back to where Wilson sat in the rear seat of the doorless, box-bodied motor car beside his wife, them both grinning with excitement, and Wilson leaned forward and whispered,

"See the birds dropping. Means the old boy has left his kill."

On the far bank of the stream Macomber could see, above the trees, vultures circling and plummeting down.

"Chances are he'll come to drink along here," Wilson whispered. "Before he goes to lay up. Keep an eye out."

They were driving slowly along the high bank of the stream which here cut deeply to its boulder-filled bed, and they wound in and out through big trees as they drove. Macomber was watching the opposite bank when he felt Wilson take hold of his arm. The car stopped.

"There he is," he heard the whisper. "Ahead and to the right. Get out and take him. He's a marvellous lion."

Macomber saw the lion now. He was standing almost broadside, his great head up and turned toward them. The early morning breeze that blew toward them was just stirring his dark mane, and the lion looked huge, silhouetted on the rise of bank in the gray morning light, his shoulders heavy, his barrel of a body bulking smoothly.

"How far is he?" asked Macomber, raising his rifle.

"About seventy-five. Get out and take him."

"Why not shoot from where I am?"

"You don't shoot them from cars," he heard Wilson saying in his ear. "Get out. He's not going to stay there all day."

Macomber stepped out of the curved opening at the side of the front seat, onto the step and down onto the ground. The lion still stood looking majestically and coolly toward this object that his eyes only showed in silhouette, bulking like some super-rhino. There was no man smell carried toward him and he watched the object, moving his great head a little from side to side. Then watching the object, not afraid, but hesitating before going down the bank to drink with such a thing opposite him, he saw a man figure detach itself from it and he turned his heavy head and swung away toward the cover of the trees as he heard a cracking crash and felt the slam of a .30–06 220-grain solid bullet that bit his flank and ripped in sudden hot scalding nausea through his stomach. He trotted, heavy, big-footed, swinging wounded full-bellied, through the trees toward the tall grass and cover, and the crash came again to go past him ripping the air apart. Then it crashed again and he felt the blow as it hit his lower ribs and ripped on through, blood sudden hot and frothy in his mouth, and he galloped toward the high grass

31 **to rip** to tear – **to scald** [skɔ:ld] to burn as with boiling water – 32 **nausea** [ˈnɔ:zjə] feeling of sickness

where he could crouch and not be seen and make them bring the crashing thing close enough so he could make a rush and get the man that held it.

Macomber had not thought how the lion felt as he got out of the car. He only knew his hands were shaking and as he walked away from the car it was almost impossible for him to make his legs move. They were stiff in the thighs, but he could feel the muscles fluttering. He raised the rifle, sighted on the junction of the lion's head and shoulders and pulled the trigger. Nothing happened though he pulled until he thought his finger would break. Then he knew he had the safety on and as he lowered the rifle to move the safety over he moved another frozen pace forward, and the lion seeing his silhouette now clear of the silhouette of the car, turned and started off at a trot, and, as Macomber fired, he heard a whunk that meant that the bullet was home; but the lion kept on going. Macomber shot again and everyone saw the bullet throw a spout of dirt beyond the trotting lion. He shot again, remembering to lower his aim, and they all heard the bullet hit, and the lion went into a gallop and was in the tall grass before he had the bolt pushed forward.

Macomber stood there feeling sick at his stomach, his hands that held the Springfield still cocked, shaking, and his wife and Robert Wilson were standing by him. Beside him too were the two gun-bearers chattering in Wakamba.

"I hit him," Macomber said. "I hit him twice."

"You gut-shot him and you hit him somewhere forward," Wilson said without enthusiasm. The gun-bearers looked very grave. They were silent now.

"You may have killed him," Wilson went on. "We'll have to wait a while before we go in to find out."

"What do you mean?"

"Let him get sick before we follow him up."

"Oh," said Macomber.

"He's a hell of a fine lion," Wilson said cheerfully. "He's gotten into a bad place though."

"Why is it bad?"

"Can't see him until you're on him."

"Oh," said Macomber.

"Come on," said Wilson. "The Memsahib can stay here in the car. We'll go to have a look at the blood spoor."

16 **bolt** sliding part in a rifle (Verschluß)

"Stay here, Margot," Macomber said to his wife. His mouth was very dry and it was hard for him to talk.

"Why?" she asked.

"Wilson says to."

"We're going to have a look," Wilson said. "You stay here. You can see even better from here."

"All right."

Wilson spoke in Swahili to the driver. He nodded and said, "Yes, Bwana."

Then they went down the steep bank and across the stream, climbing over and around the boulders and up the other bank, pulling up by some projecting roots, and along it until they found where the lion had been trotting when Macomber first shot. There was dark blood on the short grass that the gun-bearers pointed out with grass stems, and that ran away behind the river bank trees.

"What do we do?" asked Macomber.

"Not much choice," said Wilson. "We can't bring the car over. Bank's too steep. We'll let him stiffen up a bit and then you and I'll go in and have a look for him."

"Can't we set the grass on fire?" Macomber asked.

"Too green."

"Can't we send beaters?"

Wilson looked at him appraisingly. "Of course we can," he said. "But it's just a touch murderous. You see we know the lion's wounded. You can drive an unwounded lion – he'll move on ahead of a noise – but a wounded lion's going to charge. You can't see him until you're right on him. He'll make himself perfectly flat in cover you wouldn't think would hide a hare. You can't very well send boys in there to that sort of a show. Somebody bound to get mauled."

"What about the gun-bearers?"

"Oh, they'll go with us. It's their *shauri*. You see, they signed on for it. They don't look too happy though, do they?"

"I don't want to go in there," said Macomber. It was out before he knew he'd said it.

"Neither do I," said Wilson very cheerily. "Really no choice though." Then, as an afterthought, he glanced at Macomber and saw suddenly how he was trembling and the pitiful look on his face.

23 **to appraise** to judge carefully – 29 **to maul** to injure by rough or brutal handling

"You don't have to go in, of course," he said. "That's what I'm hired for, you know. That's why I'm so expensive."

"You mean you'd go in by yourself? Why not leave him there?"

Robert Wilson, whose entire occupation had been with the lion and the problem he presented, and who had not been thinking about Macomber except to note that he was rather windy, suddenly felt as though he had opened the wrong door in a hotel and seen something shameful.

"What do you mean?"

"Why not just leave him?"

"You mean pretend to ourselves he hasn't been hit?"

"No. Just drop it."

"It isn't done."

"Why not?"

"For one thing, he's certain to be suffering. For another, someone else might run onto him."

"I see."

"But you don't have to have anything to do with it."

"I'd like to," Macomber said. "I'm just scared, you know."

"I'll go ahead when we go in," Wilson said, "with Kongoni tracking. You keep behind me and a little to one side. Chances are we'll hear him growl. If we see him we'll both shoot. Don't worry about anything. I'll keep you backed up. As a matter of fact, you know, perhaps you'd better not go. It might be much better. Why don't you go over and join the Memsahib while I just get it over with?"

"No, I want to go."

"All right," said Wilson. "But don't go in if you don't want to. This is my *shauri* now, you know."

"I want to go," said Macomber.

They sat under a tree and smoked.

"Want to go back and speak to the Memsahib while we're waiting?" Wilson asked.

"No."

"I'll just step back and tell her to be patient."

"Good," said Macomber. He sat there, sweating under his arms, his mouth dry, his stomach hollow feeling, wanting to find courage to tell Wilson to go on and finish off the lion without him. He could not know that Wilson was furious because he had not noticed the state he was in earlier and sent him back to his wife. While he sat there Wilson came up. "I have

6 **windy** *slang* nervous – 12 **It isn't done** one does not do that sort of thing

your big gun," he said. "Take it. We've given him time, I think. Come on."

Macomber took the big gun and Wilson said:

"Keep behind me and about five yards to the right and do exactly as I tell you." Then he spoke in Swahili to the two gun-bearers who looked the picture of gloom.

"Let's go," he said.

"Could I have a drink of water?" Macomber asked. Wilson spoke to the older gun-bearer, who wore a canteen on his belt, and the man unbuckled it, unscrewed the top and handed it to Macomber, who took it noticing how heavy it seemed and how hairy and shoddy the felt covering was in his hand. He raised it to drink and looked ahead at the high grass with the flat-topped trees behind it. A breeze was blowing toward them and the grass rippled gently in the wind. He looked at the gun-bearer and he could see the gun-bearer was suffering too with fear.

Thirty-five yards into the grass the big lion lay flattened out along the ground. His ears were back and his only movement was a slight twitching up and down of his long, black-tufted tail. He had turned at bay as soon as he had reached this cover and he was sick with the wound through his full belly, and weakening with the wound through his lungs that brought a thin foamy red to his mouth each time he breathed. His flanks were wet and hot and flies were on the little openings the solid bullets had made in his tawny hide, and his big yellow eyes, narrowed with hate, looked straight ahead, only blinking when the pain came as he breathed, and his claws dug in the soft baked earth. All of him, pain, sickness, hatred and all of his remaining strength, was tightening into an absolute concentration for a rush. He could hear the men talking and he waited, gathering all of himself into this preparation for a charge as soon as the men would come into the grass. As he heard their voices his tail stiffened to twitch up and down, and, as they came into the edge of the grass, he made a coughing grunt and charged.

Kongoni, the old gun-bearer, in the lead watching the blood spoor, Wilson watching the grass for any movement, his big gun ready, the second gun-bearer looking ahead and listening, Macomber close to Wilson, his rifle cocked, they had just moved into the grass when Macomber heard the blood-choked coughing grunt, and saw the swishing rush in the grass. The next thing he knew he was running; running wildly, in panic in the open, running toward the stream.

He heard the *ca-ra-wong!* of Wilson's big rifle, and again in a second crashing *carawong!* and turning saw the lion, horrible-looking now, with half

17 **at bay** facing one's attacker

his head seeming to be gone, crawling toward Wilson in the edge of the tall grass while the red-faced man worked the bolt on the short ugly rifle and aimed carefully as another blasting *carawong!* came from the muzzle, and the crawling, heavy, yellow bulk of the lion stiffened and the huge, mutilated head slid forward and Macomber, standing by himself in the clearing where he had run, holding a loaded rifle, while two black men and a white man looked back at him in contempt, knew the lion was dead. He came toward Wilson, his tallness all seeming a naked reproach, and Wilson looked at him and said:

"Want to take pictures?"

"No," he said.

That was all anyone had said until they reached the motor car. Then Wilson had said:

"Hell of a fine lion. Boys will skin him out. We might as well stay here in the shade."

Macomber's wife had not looked at him nor he at her and he had sat by her in the back seat with Wilson sitting in the front seat. Once he had reached over and taken his wife's hand without looking at her and she had removed her hand from his. Looking across the stream to where the gun-bearers were skinning out the lion he could see that she had been able to see the whole thing. While they sat there his wife had reached forward and put her hand on Wilson's shoulder. He turned and she had leaned forward over the low seat and kissed him on the mouth.

"Oh, I say," said Wilson, going redder than his natural baked color.

"Mr. Robert Wilson," she said. "The beautiful red-faced Mr. Robert Wilson."

Then she sat down beside Macomber again and looked away across the stream to where the lion lay, with uplifted, white-muscled, tendon-marked naked forearms, and white bloating belly, as the black men fleshed away the skin. Finally the gun-bearers brought the skin over, wet and heavy, and climbed in behind with it, rolling it up before they got in, and the motor car started. No one had said anything more until they were back in camp.

That was the story of the lion. Macomber did not know how the lion had felt before he started his rush, nor during it when the unbelievable smash of the .505 with a muzzle velocity of two tons had hit him in the mouth, nor what kept him coming after that, when the second ripping crash had

4 **to mutilate** to disfigure by cutting off or destroying a part – 7 **in contempt** looking down on (verächtlich) – 8 **reproach** [rɪ'prəʊtʃ] moral accusation

smashed his hind quarters and he had come crawling on toward the crashing, blasting thing that had destroyed him. Wilson knew something about it and only expressed it by saying, "Damned fine lion," but Macomber did not know how Wilson felt about things either. He did not know how his wife felt except that she was through with him.

His wife had been through with him before but it never lasted. He was very wealthy, and would be much wealthier, and he knew she would not leave him ever now. That was one of the few things that he really knew. He knew about that, about motor cycles – that was earliest – about motor cars, about duck-shooting, about fishing, trout, salmon and big-sea, about sex in books, many books, too many books, about all court games, about dogs, not much about horses, about hanging on to his money, about most of the other things his world dealt in, and about his wife not leaving him. His wife had been a great beauty and she was still a great beauty in Africa, but she was not a great enough beauty any more at home to be able to leave him and better herself and she knew it and he knew it. She had missed the chance to leave him and he knew it. If he had been better with women she would probably have started to worry about him getting another new, beautiful wife; but she knew too much about him to worry about him either. Also, he had always had a great tolerance which seemed the nicest thing about him if it were not the most sinister.

All in all they were known as a comparatively happily married couple, one of those whose disruption is often rumored but never occurs, and as the society columnist put it, they were adding more than a spice of *adventure* to their much envied and ever-enduring *Romance* by a *Safari* in what was known as *Darkest Africa* until the Martin Johnsons lighted it on so many silver screens where they were pursuing *Old Simba* the lion, the buffalo, *Tembo* the elephant and as well collecting specimens for the Museum of Natural History. This same columnist had reported them *on the verge* at least three times in the past and they had been. But they always made it up. They had a sound basis of union. Margot was too beautiful for Macomber to divorce her and Macomber had too much money for Margot ever to leave him.

It was now about three o'clock in the morning and Francis Macomber,

5 **to be through with s.o.** to be at the end of all relations or dealings with s.o. – 21 **sinister** [ˈsɪnɪstə] dark, suggesting or threatening evil – 29 **verge** edge – **on the verge** *here:* on the point of getting divorced – 30 **to make it up with s.o.** to end a quarrel

who had been asleep a little while after he had stopped thinking about the lion, wakened and then slept again, woke suddenly, frightened in a dream of the bloody-headed lion standing over him, and listening while his heart pounded, he realized that his wife was not in the other cot in the tent. He lay awake with that knowledge for two hours.

At the end of that time his wife came into the tent, lifted her mosquito bar and crawled cozily into bed.

"Where have you been?" Macomber asked in the darkness.

"Hello," she said. "Are you awake?"

"Where have you been?"

"I just went out to get a breath of air."

"You did, like hell."

"What do you want me to say, darling?"

"Where have you been?"

"Out to get a breath of air."

"That's a new name for it. You *are* a bitch."

"Well, you're a coward."

"All right," he said. "What of it?"

"Nothing as far as I'm concerned. But please let's not talk, darling, because I'm very sleepy."

"You think that I'll take anything."

"I know you will, sweet."

"Well, I won't."

"Please, darling, let's not talk. I'm so very sleepy."

"There wasn't going to be any of that. You promised there wouldn't be."

"Well, there is now," she said sweetly.

"You said if we made this trip that there would be none of that. You promised."

"Yes, darling. That's the way I meant it to be. But the trip was spoiled yesterday. We don't have to talk about it, do we?"

"You don't wait long when you have an advantage, do you?"

"Please let's not talk. I'm so sleepy, darling."

"I'm going to talk."

"Don't mind me then, because I'm going to sleep." And she did.

At breakfast they were all three at the table before daylight and Francis Macomber found that, of all the many men that he had hated, he hated Robert Wilson the most.

"Sleep well?" Wilson asked in his throaty voice, filling a pipe.

"Did you?"

"Topping," the white hunter told him.

You bastard, thought Macomber, you insolent bastard.

So she woke him when she came in, Wilson thought, looking at them both with his flat, cold eyes. Well, why doesn't he keep his wife where she belongs? What does he think I am, a bloody plaster saint? Let him keep her where she belongs. It's his own fault.

"Do you think we'll find buffalo?" Margot asked, pushing away a dish of apricots.

"Chance of it," Wilson said and smiled at her. "Why don't you stay in camp?"

"Not for anything," she told him.

"Why not order her to stay in camp?" Wilson said to Macomber.

"You order her," said Macomber coldly.

"Let's not have any ordering, nor," turning to Macomber, "any silliness, Francis," Margot said quite pleasantly.

"Are you ready to start?" Macomber asked.

"Any time," Wilson told him. "Do you want the Memsahib to go?"

"Does it make any difference whether I do or not?"

The hell with it, thought Robert Wilson. The utter complete hell with it. So this is what it's going to be like. Well, this is what it's going to be like, then.

"Makes no difference," he said.

"You're sure you wouldn't like to stay in camp with her yourself and let me go out and hunt the buffalo?" Macomber asked.

"Can't do that," said Wilson. "Wouldn't talk rot if I were you."

"I'm not talking rot. I'm disgusted."

"Bad word, disgusted."

"Francis, will you please try to speak sensibly?" his wife said.

"I speak too damned sensibly," Macomber said. "Did you ever eat such filthy food?"

"Something wrong with the food?" asked Wilson quietly.

"No more than with everything else."

"I'd pull yourself together, laddybuck," Wilson said very quietly. "There's a boy waits at table that understands a little English."

"The hell with him."

Wilson stood up and puffing on his pipe strolled away, speaking a few words in Swahili to one of the gun-bearers who was standing waiting for him. Macomber and his wife sat on at the table. He was staring at his coffee cup.

"If you make a scene I'll leave you, darling," Margot said quietly.

"No, you won't."

"You can try it and see."

"You won't leave me."

"No," she said. "I won't leave you and you'll behave yourself."

"Behave myself? That's a way to talk. Behave myself."

"Yes. Behave yourself."

"Why don't *you* try behaving?"

"I've tried it so long. So very long."

"I hate that red-faced swine," Macomber said. "I loathe the sight of him."

"He's really *very* nice."

"Oh, *shut up*," Macomber almost shouted. Just then the car came up and stopped in front of the dining tent and the driver and the two gun-bearers got out. Wilson walked over and looked at the husband and wife sitting there at the table.

"Going shooting?" he asked.

"Yes," said Macomber, standing up. "Yes."

"Better bring a woolly. It will be cool in the car," Wilson said.

"I'll get my leather jacket," Margot said.

"The boy has it," Wilson told her. He climbed into the front with the driver and Francis Macomber and his wife sat, not speaking, in the back seat. Hope the silly beggar doesn't take a notion to blow the back of my head off, Wilson thought to himself. Women *are* a nuisance on safari.

The car was grinding down to cross the river at a pebbly ford in the gray daylight and then climbed, angling up the steep bank, where Wilson had ordered a way shovelled out the day before so they could reach the parklike wooded rolling country on the far side.

It was a good morning, Wilson thought. There was a heavy dew and as the wheels went through the grass and low bushes he could smell the odor of the crushed fronds. It was an odor like verbena and he liked this early morning smell of the dew, the crushed bracken and the look of the tree trunks showing black through the early morning mist, as the car made its way through the untracked, parklike country. He had put the two in the back seat out of his mind now and was thinking about buffalo. The buffalo that he was after stayed in the daytime in a thick swamp where it was impossible to get a shot, but in the night they fed out into an open stretch of country and if he could come between them and their swamp with the car, Macomber would have a good chance at them in the open. He did not want to hunt buff with Macomber in thick cover. He did not want to hunt buff or any-

8 **to loathe** to feel disgust for – 28 **to crush** to press s. th. till it breaks

thing else with Macomber at all, but he was a professional hunter and he had hunted with some rare ones in his time. If they got buff today there would only be rhino to come and the poor man would have gone through his dangerous game and things might pick up. He'd have nothing more to do with the woman and Macomber would get over that too. He must have gone through plenty of that before by the look of things. Poor beggar. He must have a way of getting over it. Well, it was the poor sod's own bloody fault.

He, Robert Wilson, carried a double size cot on safari to accommodate any windfalls he might receive. He had hunted for a certain clientele, the international, fast, sporting set, where the women did not feel they were getting their money's worth unless they had shared that cot with the white hunter. He despised them when he was away from them although he liked some of them well enough at the time, but he made his living by them; and their standards were his standards as long as they were hiring him.

They were his standards in all except the shooting. He had his own standards about the killing and they could live up to them or get someone else to hunt for them. He knew, too, that they all respected him for this. This Macomber was an odd one though. Damned if he wasn't. Now the wife. Well, the wife. Yes, the wife. Hm, the wife. Well he'd dropped all that. He looked around at them. Macomber sat grim and furious. Margot smiled at him. She looked younger today, more innocent and fresher and not so professionally beautiful. What's in her heart God knows, Wilson thought. She hadn't talked much last night. At that it was a pleasure to see her.

The motor car climbed up a slight rise and went on through the trees and then out into a grassy prairie-like opening and kept in the shelter of the trees along the edge, the driver going slowly and Wilson looking carefully out across the prairie and all along its far side. He stopped the car and studied the opening with his field glasses. Then he motioned to the driver to go on and the car moved slowly along, the driver avoiding wart-hog holes and driving around the mud castles ants had built. Then, looking across the opening, Wilson suddenly turned and said,

"By God, there they are!"

And looking where he pointed, while the car jumped forward and Wilson spoke in rapid Swahili to the driver, Macomber saw three huge, black animals looking almost cylindrical in their long heaviness, like big black tank

4 **to pick up** to get better – 10 **windfall** unexpected lucky event – 13 **to despise** to be contemptuous of, to look down on

cars, moving at a gallop across the far edge of the open prairie. They moved at a stiff-necked, stiff-bodied gallop and he could see the upswept wide black horns on their heads as they galloped heads out; the heads not moving.

"They're three old bulls," Wilson said. "We'll cut them off before they get to the swamp."

The car was going a wild forty-five miles an hour across the open and as Macomber watched, the buffalo got bigger and bigger until he could see the gray, hairless, scabby look of one huge bull and how his neck was a part of his shoulders and the shiny black of his horns as he galloped a little behind the others that were strung out in that steady plunging gait; and then, the car swaying as though it had just jumped a road, they drew up close and he could see the plunging hugeness of the bull, and the dust in his sparsely haired hide, the wide boss of horn and his outstretched, wide-nostrilled muzzle, and he was raising his rifle when Wilson shouted, "Not from the car, you fool!" and he had no fear, only hatred of Wilson, while the brakes clamped on and the car skidded, plowing sideways to an almost stop and Wilson was out on one side and he on the other, stumbling as his feet hit the still speeding-by of the earth, and then he was shooting at the bull as he moved away, hearing the bullets whunk into him, emptying his rifle at him as he moved steadily away, finally remembering to get his shots forward into the shoulder, and as he fumbled to re-load, he saw the bull was down. Down on his knees, his big head tossing, and seeing the other two still galloping he shot at the leader and hit him. He shot again and missed and he heard the *carawonging* roar as Wilson shot and saw the leading bull slide forward onto his nose.

"Get that other," Wilson said. "Now you're shooting!"

But the other bull was moving steadily at the same gallop and he missed, throwing a spout of dirt, and Wilson missed and the dust rose in a cloud and Wilson shouted, "Come on. He's too far!" and grabbed his arm and they were in the car again, Macomber and Wilson hanging on the sides and rocketing swayingly over the uneven ground, drawing up on the steady, plunging, heavy-necked, straight-moving gallop of the bull.

They were behind him and Macomber was filling his rifle, dropping shells onto the ground, jamming it, clearing the jam, then they were almost up with

10 **to string out** to space out at even intervals along a line – **to plunge** to move forward and downward very quickly – **gait** manner of walking or running – 11 **to sway** to move from side to side – 13 **boss** (Buckel, Wulst) – 17 **to stumble** nearly to fall – 21 **to fumble** to use one's hands awkwardly

the bull when Wilson yelled "Stop," and the car skidded so that it almost swung over and Macomber fell forward onto his feet, slammed his bolt forward and fired as far forward as he could aim into the galloping, rounded black back, aimed and shot again, then again, then again, and the bullets, all of them hitting, had no effect on the buffalo that he could see. Then Wilson shot, the roar deafening him, and he could see the bull stagger. Macomber shot again, aiming carefully, and down he came, onto his knees.

"All right," Wilson said. "Nice work. That's the three."

Macomber felt a drunken elation.

"How many times did you shoot?" he asked.

"Just three," Wilson said. "You killed the first bull. The biggest one. I helped you finish the other two. Afraid they might have got into cover. You had them killed. I was just mopping up a little. You shot damn well."

"Let's go to the car," said Macomber. "I want a drink."

"Got to finish off that buff first," Wilson told him. The buffalo was on his knees and he jerked his head furiously and bellowed in pig-eyed, roaring rage as they came toward him.

"Watch he doesn't get up," Wilson said. Then, "Get a little broadside and take him in the neck just behind the ear."

Macomber aimed carefully at the center of the huge, jerking, rage-driven neck and shot. At the shot the head dropped forward.

"That does it," said Wilson. "Got the spine. They're a hell of a looking thing, aren't they?"

"Let's get the drink," said Macomber. In his life he had never felt so good.

In the car Macomber's wife sat very white-faced. "You were marvellous, darling," she said to Macomber. "What a ride."

"Was it rough?" Wilson asked.

"It was frightful. I've never been more frightened in my life."

"Let's all have a drink," Macomber said.

"By all means," said Wilson. "Give it to the Memsahib." She drank the neat whisky from the flask and shuddered a little when she swallowed. She handed the flask to Macomber who handed it to Wilson.

"It was frightfully exciting," she said. "It's given me a dreadful headache. I didn't know you were allowed to shoot them from cars though."

"No one shot from cars," said Wilson coldly.

"I mean chase them from cars."

"Wouldn't ordinarily," Wilson said. "Seemed sporting enough to me

9 **elation** feeling of joy – 13 **to mop up** to clean or tidy up

though while we were doing it. Taking more chance driving that way across the plain full of holes and one thing and another than hunting on foot. Buffalo could have charged us each time we shot if he liked. Gave him every chance. Wouldn't mention it to anyone though. It's illegal if that's what you mean."

"It seemed very unfair to me," Margot said, "chasing those big helpless things in a motor car."

"Did it?" said Wilson.

"What would happen if they heard about it in Nairobi?"

"I'd lose my licence for one thing. Other unpleasantnesses," Wilson said, taking a drink from the flask. "I'd be out of business."

"Really?"

"Yes, really."

"Well," said Macomber, and he smiled for the first time all day. "Now she has something on you."

"You have such a pretty way of putting things, Francis," Margot Macomber said. Wilson looked at them both. If a four-letter man marries a five-letter woman, he was thinking, what number of letters would their children be? What he said was, "We lost a gun-bearer. Did you notice it?"

"My God, no," Macomber said.

"Here he comes," Wilson said. "He's all right. He must have fallen off when we left the first bull."

Approaching them was the middle-aged gun-bearer, limping along in his knitted cap, khaki tunic, shorts and rubber sandals, gloomy-faced and disgusted looking. As he came up he called out to Wilson in Swahili and they all saw the change in the white hunter's face.

"What does he say?" asked Margot.

"He says the first bull got up and went into the bush," Wilson said with no expression in his voice.

"Oh," said Macomber blankly.

"Then it's going to be just like the lion," said Margot, full of anticipation.

"It's not going to be a damned bit like the lion," Wilson told her. "Did you want another drink, Macomber?"

"Thanks, yes," Macomber said. He expected the feeling he had had about the lion to come back but it did not. For the first time in his life he really felt

15 **she has something on you** she knows s.th. about you which she can use against you – 17 **five-letter woman** *variation on* "four-letter man", see above p. 44 l. 33; the five-letter word Wilson is thinking of is probably "bitch"

wholly without fear. Instead of fear he had a feeling of definite elation.

"We'll go and have a look at the second bull," Wilson said. "I'll tell the driver to put the car in the shade."

"What are you going to do?" asked Margaret Macomber.

"Take a look at the buff," Wilson said.

"I'll come."

"Come along."

The three of them walked over to where the second buffalo bulked blackly in the open, head forward on the grass, the massive horns swung wide.

"He's a very good head," Wilson said. "That's close to a fifty-inch spread."

Macomber was looking at him with delight.

"He's hateful looking," said Margot. "Can't we go into the shade?"

"Of course," Wilson said. "Look," he said to Macomber, and pointed. "See that patch of bush?"

"Yes."

"That's where the first bull went in. The gun-bearer said when he fell off the bull was down. He was watching us helling along and the other two buff galloping. When he looked up there was the bull up and looking at him. Gun-bearer ran like hell and the bull went off slowly into that bush."

"Can we go in after him now?" asked Macomber eagerly.

Wilson looked at him appraisingly. Damned if this isn't a strange one, he thought. Yesterday he's scared sick and today he's a ruddy fire eater.

"No, we'll give him a while."

"Let's please go into the shade," Margot said. Her face was white and she looked ill.

They made their way to the car where it stood under a single, wide-spreading tree and all climbed in.

"Chances are he's dead in there," Wilson remarked. "After a little we'll have a look."

Macomber felt a wild unreasonable happiness that he had never known before.

"By God, that was a chase," he said. "I've never felt any such feeling. Wasn't it marvellous, Margot?"

"I hated it."

"Why?"

"I hated it," she said bitterly. "I loathed it."

"You know I don't think I'd ever be afraid of anything again," Macomber said to Wilson. "Something happened in me after we first saw the buff and started after him. Like a dam bursting. It was pure excitement."

"Cleans out your liver," said Wilson. "Damn funny things happen to people."

Macomber's face was shining. "You know something did happen to me," he said. "I feel absolutely different."

His wife said nothing and eyed him strangely. She was sitting far back in the seat and Macomber was sitting forward talking to Wilson who turned sideways talking over the back of the front seat.

"You know, I'd like to try another lion," Macomber said. "I'm really not afraid of them now. After all, what can they do to you?"

"That's it," said Wilson. "Worst one can do is kill you. How does it go? Shakespeare. Damned good. See if I can remember. Oh, damned good. Used to quote it to myself at one time. Let's see. 'By my troth, I care not; a man can die but once; we owe God a death and let it go which way it will he that dies this year is quit for the next.' Damned fine, eh?"

He was very embarrassed, having brought out this thing he had lived by, but he had seen men come of age before and it always moved him. It was not a matter of their twenty-first birthday.

It had taken a strange chance of hunting, a sudden precipitation into action without opportunity for worrying beforehand, to bring this about with Macomber, but regardless of how it had happened it had most certainly happened. Look at the beggar now, Wilson thought. It's that some of them stay little boys so long, Wilson thought. Sometimes all their lives. Their figures stay boyish when they're fifty. The great American boy-men. Damned strange people. But he liked this Macomber now. Damned strange fellow. Probably meant the end of cuckoldry too. Well, that would be a damned good thing. Damned good thing. Beggar had probably been afraid all his life. Don't know what started it. But over now. Hadn't had time to be afraid with the buff. That and being angry too. Motor car too. Motor cars made it familiar. Be a damn fire eater now. He'd seen it in the war work the same way. More of a change than any loss of virginity. Fear gone like an operation. Something else grew in its place. Main thing a man had. Made him into a man. Women knew it too. No bloody fear.

From the far corner of the seat Margaret Macomber looked at the two of

1 **liver** traditionally the seat of courage; to be "yellow-livered" is to be a coward – 12 **by my troth** ['trəʊθ] by my honour; Wilson is quoting Shakespeare – 16 **to come of age** to reach the age of maturity – 25 **cuckoldry** ['kʌkəldrɪ] the condition of a husband whose wife is unfaithful – 30 **virginity** [vɜː'dʒɪnɪtɪ] (Jungfräulichkeit)

them. There was no change in Wilson. She saw Wilson as she had seen him the day before when she had first realized what his great talent was. But she saw the change in Francis Macomber now.

"Do you have that feeling of happiness about what's going to happen?" Macomber asked, still exploring his new wealth.

"You're not supposed to mention it," Wilson said, looking in the other's face. "Much more fashionable to say you're scared. Mind you, you'll be scared too, plenty of times."

"But you *have* a feeling of happiness about action to come?"

"Yes," said Wilson. "There's that. Doesn't do to talk too much about all this. Talk the whole thing away. No pleasure in anything if you mouth it up too much."

"You're both talking rot," said Margot. "Just because you've chased some helpless animals in a motor car you talk like heroes."

"Sorry," said Wilson. "I have been gassing too much." She's worried about it already, he thought.

"If you don't know what we're talking about why not keep out of it?" Macomber asked his wife.

"You've gotten awfully brave, awfully suddenly," his wife said contemptuously, but her contempt was not secure. She was very afraid of something.

Macomber laughed, a very natural hearty laugh. "You know I *have*," he said. "I really have."

"Isn't it sort of late?" Margot said bitterly. Because she had done the best she could for many years back and the way they were together now was no one person's fault.

"Not for me," said Macomber.

Margot said nothing but sat back in the corner of the seat.

"Do you think we've given him time enough?" Macomber asked Wilson cheerfully.

"We might have a look," Wilson said. "Have you any solids left?"

"The gun-bearer has some."

Wilson called in Swahili and the older gun-bearer, who was skinning out one of the heads, straightened up, pulled a box of solids out of his pocket and brought them over to Macomber, who filled his magazine and put the remaining shells in his pocket.

10 **doesn't do** it is not good – 11 **to mouth s.th. up** [maʊð] to talk about s.th. too much – 15 **to gas** *colloquial* to talk a lot without really saying anything

"You might as well shoot the Springfield," Wilson said. "You're used to it. We'll leave the Mannlicher in the car with the Memsahib. Your gun-bearer can carry your heavy gun. I've this damned cannon. Now let me tell you about them." He had saved this until the last because he did not want to worry Macomber. "When a buff comes he comes with his head high and thrust straight out. The boss of the horns covers any sort of a brain shot. The only shot is straight into the nose. The only other shot is into his chest or, if you're to one side, into the neck or the shoulders. After they've been hit once they take a hell of a lot of killing. Don't try anything fancy. Take the easiest shot there is. They've finished skinning out that head now. Should we get started?"

He called to the gun-bearers, who came up wiping their hands, and the older one got into the back.

"I'll only take Kongoni," Wilson said. "The other can watch to keep the birds away."

As the car moved slowly across the open space toward the island of brushy trees that ran in a tongue of foliage along a dry water course that cut the open swale, Macomber felt his heart pounding and his mouth was dry again, but it was excitement, not fear.

"Here's where he went in," Wilson said. Then to the gunbearer in Swahili, "Take the blood spoor."

The car was parallel to the patch of bush. Macomber, Wilson and the gun-bearer got down. Macomber, looking back, saw his wife, with the rifle by her side, looking at him. He waved to her and she did not wave back.

The brush was very thick ahead and the ground was dry. The middle-aged gun-bearer was sweating heavily and Wilson had his hat down over his eyes and his red neck showed just ahead of Macomber. Suddenly the gun-bearer said something in Swahili to Wilson and ran forward.

"He's dead in there," Wilson said. "Good work," and he turned to grip Macomber's hand and as they shook hands, grinning at each other, the gun-bearer shouted wildly and they saw him coming out of the bush sideways, fast as a crab, and the bull coming, nose out, mouth tight closed, blood dripping, massive head straight out, coming in a charge, his little pig eyes bloodshot as he looked at them. Wilson, who was ahead was kneeling shooting, and Macomber, as he fired, unhearing his shot in the roaring of Wilson's gun, saw fragments like slate burst from the huge boss of the horns, and the head jerked, he shot again at the wide nostrils and saw the horns jolt again and fragments fly, and he did not see Wilson now and, aiming carefully, shot

18 **to pound** to beat heavily

again with the buffalo's huge bulk almost on him and his rifle almost level with the on-coming head, nose out, and he could see the little wicked eyes and the head started to lower and he felt a sudden white-hot, blinding flash explode inside his head and that was all he ever felt.

Wilson had ducked to one side to get in a shoulder shot. Macomber had stood solid and shot for the nose, shooting a touch high each time and hitting the heavy horns, splintering and chipping them like hitting a slate roof, and Mrs. Macomber, in the car, had shot at the buffalo with the 6.5 Mannlicher as it seemed about to gore Macomber and had hit her husband about two inches up and a little to one side of the base of his skull.

Francis Macomber lay now, face down, not two yards from where the buffalo lay on his side and his wife knelt over him with Wilson beside her.

"I wouldn't turn him over," Wilson said.

The woman was crying hysterically.

"I'd get back in the car," Wilson said. "Where's the rifle?"

She shook her head, her face contorted. The gun-bearer picked up the rifle.

"Leave it as it is," said Wilson. Then, "Go get Abdulla so that he may witness the manner of the accident."

He knelt down, took a handkerchief from his pocket, and spread it over Francis Macomber's crew-cropped head where it lay. The blood sank into the dry, loose earth.

Wilson stood up and saw the buffalo on his side, his legs out, his thinly-haired belly crawling with ticks. "Hell of a good bull," his brain registered automatically. "A good fifty inches, or better. Better." He called to the driver and told him to spread a blanket over the body and stay by it. Then he walked over to the motor car where the woman sat crying in the corner.

"That was a pretty thing to do," he said in a toneless voice. "He *would* have left you too."

"Stop it," she said.

"Of course it's an accident," he said. "I know that."

"Stop it," she said.

"Don't worry," he said. "There will be a certain amount of unpleasantness but I will have some photographs taken that will be very useful at the inquest. There's the testimony of the gun-bearers and the driver too. You're perfectly all right."

9 **to gore** to make a deep wound with s.th. sharp or pointed – 10 **skull** bony structure of the head – 34 **inquest** ['––] official inquiry into the cause of s.o.'s death – 35 **testimony** ['–––] statement made by a witness

"Stop it," she said.

"There's a hell of a lot to be done," he said. "And I'll have to send a truck off to the lake to wireless for a plane to take the three of us into Nairobi. Why didn't you poison him? That's what they do in England."

"Stop it. Stop it. Stop it," the woman cried.

Wilson looked at her with his flat blue eyes.

"I'm through now," he said. "I was a little angry. I'd begun to like your husband."

"Oh, please stop it," she said. "Please, please stop it."

"That's better," Wilson said. "Please is much better. Now I'll stop."

3 **to wireless** to send a message by radio

Shootism versus Sport: The Second Tanganyika Letter

There are two ways to murder a lion. One is to shoot him from a motor car, the other, to shoot him at night with a flashlight from a platform or the shelter of a thorn boma, or blind, as he comes to feed on a bait placed by the shootist or his guide. (Tourists who shoot in Africa are called shootists to distinguish them from sportsmen.) These two ways to murder lion rank, as sport, with dynamiting trout or harpooning swordfish. Yet many men who go to Africa and return to think of themselves as sportsmen and big game hunters, have killed lions from motor cars or from blinds.

The Serengeti plain is the great lion country of present day Africa and the Serengeti is a motor car proposition. The distances between water are too great for it to have been reached and hunted in the old foot safari days, and that was what preserved it. The game migrations, which are determined by the food which is produced by an often casual and unpredictable rainfall, are movements over hundreds of miles, and you may drive seventy-five or a hundred miles over a brown, dry, parched, dusty waste without seeing a head of game, to come suddenly onto a rise of green horizon broken and

3 **a blind** a screen behind which a hunter can hide – 5 **to rank with** to be on the same level as – 7 **game** wild animals which are hunted for sport – 10 **a motor car proposition** *colloquial* s.th. to be dealt with using a car – 12 **migration** [maɪˈgreɪʃn] periodical movement of animals according to the season

edged with the black of wildebeeste as far as you can see. It is because of these distances that you must use the motor car in hunting the Serengeti, since your camp must be on a water hole and the game may be over half a day's march away on the plain.

Now a lion, when you locate him in the morning after he has fed, will have only one idea if he sees a man, to get away into cover where the man will not trouble him. Until he is wounded, that lion will not be dangerous unless you come on him unexpectedly, so closely that you startle him, or unless he is on a kill and does not want to leave it.

If you approach the lion in a motor car, the lion will not see you. His eyes can only distinguish the outline or silhouette of objects, and, because it is illegal to shoot from a motor car, this object means nothing to him. If anything, since the practice of shooting a zebra and dragging it on a rope behind the motor car as a bait for lion in order to take photographs, the motor car may seem a friendly object. For a man to shoot at a lion from the protection of a motor car, where the lion cannot even see what it is that is attacking him, is not only illegal but is a cowardly way to assassinate one of the finest of all game animals.

But supposing, unexpectedly, as you are crossing the country, you see a lion and a lioness say a hundred yards from the car. They are under a thorn tree and a hundred yards behind them is a deep donga, or dry, reed-filled water course, that winds across the plain for perhaps ten miles and gives perfect cover in the daytime to all the beasts of prey that follow the game herds.

You sight the lions from the car; you look the male over and decide he is shootable. You have never killed a lion. You are allowed to kill only two lions on the Serengeti and you want a lion with a full mane, as black as possible. The white hunter says quietly:

"I believe I'd take him. We might beat him but he's a damned fine lion."

You look at the lion under the tree. He looks very close, very calm, very, very big and proudly beautiful. The lioness has flattened down on the yellow grass and is swinging her tail parallel to the ground.

"All right," says the white hunter.

You step out of the car from beside the driver on the side away from the lion, and the white hunter gets out on the same side from the seat behind you.

"Better sit down," he says. You both sit down and the car drives away.

8 **to startle** to surprise, to upset – 23 **beast of prey** an animal which kills others

As the car starts to move off you have a very different feeling about lions than you have ever had when you saw them from the motor car.

As the end of the car is past, you see that the lioness has risen and is standing so that you cannot see the lion clearly.

"Can't see him," you whisper. As you say it you see that the lions have seen you. He has turned away and is trotting off and she is still standing, the tail swinging wide.

"He'll be in the donga," the white hunter says.

You stand up to shoot and the lioness turns. The lion stops and looks back. You see his great head swing toward you, his mouth wide open and his mane blowing in the wind. You hold on his shoulder, start to flinch, correct, hold your breath and squeeze off. You don't hear the gun go off but you hear a crack like the sound of a policeman's club on a rioter's head and the lion is down.

"You've got him. Watch the lioness."

She has flattened down facing you so that you see her head, the ears back, the long yellow of her is flat out along the ground and her tail is now flailing straight up and down.

"I think she's going to come," the white hunter says. "If she comes, sit down to shoot."

"Should I bust her?" you say.

"No. Maybe she won't come. Wait till she starts to come."

You stand still and see her and beyond her the bulk of the big lion, on his side now, and finally she turns slowly and goes off and out of sight into the donga.

"In the old days," the white hunter said, "the rule was to shoot the lioness first. Damned sensible rule."

The two of you walk toward the lion with your guns ready. The car comes up and the gunbearers join you. One of them throws a stone at the lion. He doesn't move. You lower the guns and go up to him.

"You got him in the neck," the white hunter says. "Damned good shooting." There is blood coming from the thick hair of his mane where the camel flies are crawling. You regret the camel flies.

"It was a lucky one," you say.

You say nothing about having squeezed off from his shoulder, and then, suddenly, a strain is over and people are shaking your hand.

"Better keep an eye out for the old lady," the white hunter says. "Don't wander over too far that way."

11 **to hold on** *here:* to aim at – **to flinch** to draw back, as in pain or fear

You are looking at the dead lion; at his wide head and the dark shag of his mane and the long, smooth, yellow sheathed body, the muscles still twitching and running minutely under the skin. He is a fine hide and all that but he was a damned wonderful looking animal when he was alive – it was a shame he should always have had the camel flies, you think.

All right. That is the nearest to a sporting way to use a motor car after lion. Once you are on the ground and the car is gone, lion hunting is the same as it always was. If you wound the lion in any but a vital spot he will make for the shelter of the donga and then you will have to go after him. At the start, if you can shoot carefully and accurately and know where to shoot, the odds are ten to one in your favor against anything untoward happening, provided you do not have to take a running shot at first. If you wound the lion and he gets into cover it is even money you will be mauled when you go in after him. A lion can still cover one hundred yards so fast toward you that there is barely time for two aimed shots before he is on you. After he has the first bullet, there is no nervous shock to further wounds, and you have to kill him stone dead or he will keep coming.

If you shoot as you should on the Serengeti, having the car drive off as you get out, the chances are that the first shot will be a moving shot, as the lions will move off when they see the man on foot. That means that unless you are a good or a very lucky shot there will be a wounded lion and a possible charge. So do not let anyone tell you that lion shooting, if you hunt big maned lions, who, being super-fine trophies, will obviously have been hunted before and be adept at saving their hides, is no longer a sporting show. It will be exactly as dangerous as you choose to make it. The only way the danger can be removed or mitigated is by your ability to shoot, and that is as it should be. You are out to kill a lion, on foot and cleanly, not to be mauled. But you will be more of a sportsman to come back from Africa without a lion than to shoot one from the protection of a motor car, or from a blind at night when the lion is blinded by a light and cannot see his assailant.

From *By-Line: Ernest Hemingway. Selected Articles and Dispatches of Four Decades*, edited by William White, New York: Charles Scribner's Sons, 1967, pp. 162–166. This article was first published in *Esquire* in June, 1934.

11 **the odds** chances in favour or against s.th. happening – **untoward** [ˌʌntəˈwɔ:d] unfortunate – 13 **it is even money** there is an equal chance that s.th. will happen or will not happen – **to maul** [mɔ:l] to hurt, to injure – 26 **to mitigate** to make less intense or serious

Interpretation and Teaching Notes

Background

Hemingway had been planning and repeatedly postponing a hunting trip to Africa ever since 1930. His second wife's wealthy uncle, Gus Pfeiffer, had "offered to finance a safari in Kenya and Tanganyika, which would be prodigiously expensive even in the midst of the Depression."[1] For Hemingway, fishing and hunting had since his boyhood been a way of escaping from the boredom and disagreeableness of everyday life and now from such snubs as the unfavourable reviews of *Death in the Afternoon* and the unflattering description of him in Gertrude Stein's *The Autobiography of Alice B. Toklas*. In August 1933 Ernest and Pauline sailed for Europe. After spending the summer and autumn in Spain and Paris they set of from Marseilles to Mombasa, Kenya, in November. At Nairobi they hired the white hunter Philip Percival as their guide. Together with Charles Thompson and Ben Fourie they spent December to February on the Serengeti plain and in the area around the Ngorongoro Crater, southeast of Lake Victoria, hunting everything that was shootable. Hemingway found himself caught up in intense competition with Charles Thompson, childishly envious of every good trophy the other man won and boastful of everything he shot himself. In the evenings the party discussed the day's adventures and Philip Percival amused them with hunting stories. As Carlos Baker points out, one topic was of particular importance to Hemingway:

> To Ernest's mind, the most memorable of Philip's anecdotes were those that centred on the loss and recovery of nerve among his former clients. Ernest himself often discoursed on his favourite subjects of bravery and cowardice. Courage, he believed, was a matter of dignity and pride. "A coward said this pride was of no importance. Perhaps it wasn't but it was of great importance to whoever had it." A man without inner dignity was an embarrassment. Ernest knew from personal experience "what it was to be a coward and what it was to cease being a coward." Now, in the presence of actual danger, he found that he did not care what happened. "I knew that it was better to live it so that if you died you had done everything that you could do about your work and your enjoyment of life up to that minute." Philip agreed that the moment of transition from cowardice to courage was a moving experience to watch. Ernest plied him with questions. This was a significant topic.[2]

---

1 Baker 1969, p. 318.
2 Baker 1969, pp. 384–385.

Such psychological drama interested Hemingway quite as much as the actual hunting, or perhaps one should say that for him hunting was simply and essentially a psychological experience in that it allowed a man to take measure of himself. That he was also susceptible to other aspects of Africa is documented by a passage towards the end of *Green Hills of Africa* (1935):

> A continent ages quickly once we come. The natives live in harmony with it. But the foreigner destroys, cuts down the trees, drains the water, so that the water supply is altered and in a short time the soil, once the sod is turned under, is cropped out and, next, it starts to blow away as it has blown away in every old country and as I had seen it start to blow in Canada. The earth gets tired of being exploited. A country wears out quickly unless man puts back in it all his residue and that of all his beasts. When he quits using beasts and uses machines, the earth defeats him quickly. The machine can't reproduce, nor does it fertilize the soil, and it eats what he cannot raise. A country was made to be as we found it. We are the intruders and after we are dead we may have ruined it but it will still be there and we don't know what the next changes are. I suppose they all end up like Mongolia.[3]

This passage, like "Shootism versus Sport" (**70–73**), may help to understand Hemingway's attitude to the animals he hunted as just one facet of man's position in the world. One can only take as much as one gives back – in this sense Macomber's death is the price due back to the land that taught him to achieve his manhood. Africa is the ideal setting for this kind of primal encounter between man and the wild, a setting that the domesticated America that Harold Krebs encounters on his return from Europe can no longer provide.

Analysis

The main themes of this story are those which have to do with the protagonist's change of experience.[4] They are typical Hemingway themes: knowing the truth about oneself and others, the difficulty of expressing this knowledge, recognizing falseness, understanding the relationship between courage and fear, honour and disgrace. In its most general form the theme is how to determine and act according to a code of behaviour worthy of a man. As in other stories, Hemingway is concerned with the definition of what

3 Ernest Hemingway, *Green Hills of Africa,* New York 1935, pp. 284–285.

4 As opposed to "change of fortune" or "change of character". The distinction is made by R.S. Crane in "The Concept of Plot and the Plot of *Tom Jones*," in R.S. Crane, ed., *Critics and Criticism,* Chicago 1952, pp. 616–648.

constitutes the good life and what happiness consists of. So Macomber's death poses a number of questions: Why does he have to die at all? Is his death an accident or is it wilful murder? Is it a sad interruption of the protagonist's promising development or is it its culmination, beyond which he could never have progressed anyway? The protagonist's life, as emphasized by the title of the story, also raises important issues: What kind of happiness has Macomber achieved? Is such happiness worth living and dying for? Is the sketch of the Macombers' life in America meant to be representative? If so, what does the African safari contribute to a definition of life?

All kinds of interpretations, from Jungian to existentialist,[5] have been proposed and there is no point in trying to summarize them here. More accessible themes are those which do not require a particular theory as grounding. Thus the descriptions of the African bush and of its animals are a theme in themselves, expressing Hemingway's love of Creation as opposed to the falsehoods of civilization (cf. **57** 6–33).

Another aspect worth dealing with is Hemingway's narrative art. Most students will immediately recognize that this long short story is not related in chronological order. It begins *in medias res* and is interrupted by two short retrospective passages and an extended flashback. In a subtle balance, the story moves simultaneously forwards to new events and back into the past. The chart on page 141 gives a summary and a visual impression of this, showing the narrative sequence from top to bottom and the chronological sequence from left to right. The main events cover a whole day and night, and the morning of the following day, with a general summary of the past prior to these one and a half days given in **57** 6–33. As the brackets on the far right of the chart show, the story consists of four distinct episodes, of which II and III occur in the past and I and IV in the present. For clarity's sake flashbacks and retrospective passages are assigned Arabic numerals (1–3) in the left-hand column, whereas the parts in the narrative present are marked by capital letters (A–G). There are ten parts in all.

As the chart suggests, the whole action of the story is dependent on "the story of the lion", as the narrator puts it (**56** 33). A simple blackboard sketch can demonstrate this (see p. 142).

5 The Jungian approach is represented by Joseph DeFalco, *The Hero in Hemingway's Short Stories,* Pittsburgh 1963. Explicitly existentialist is John Killinger, *Hemingway and the Dead Gods: A Study in Existentialism,* Lexington 1960.

Sequence and Chronology

part	past	first day: morning	first day: afternoon	first day: night	second day: morning	
A			**41** 1 – **42** 2			I: after the lion hunt
1		**42** 3–11				II: the story of the lion
B			**42** 12 – **47** 27			I: after the lion hunt
C			**47** 28 – **48** 19			I: after the lion hunt
D				**48** 20–27		II: the story of the lion
2		**48** 28 – **57** 5				II: the story of the lion
3	**57** 6–33					III: the Macombers' past
E					**57** 34 – **58** 34	IV: the buffalo hunt
F					**58** 35 – **60** 21	IV: the buffalo hunt
Ga					**60** 22 – **64** 22	IV: the buffalo hunt
Gb					**64** 23 – **67** 27	IV: the buffalo hunt
Gc					**67** 28 – **70** 10	IV: the buffalo hunt

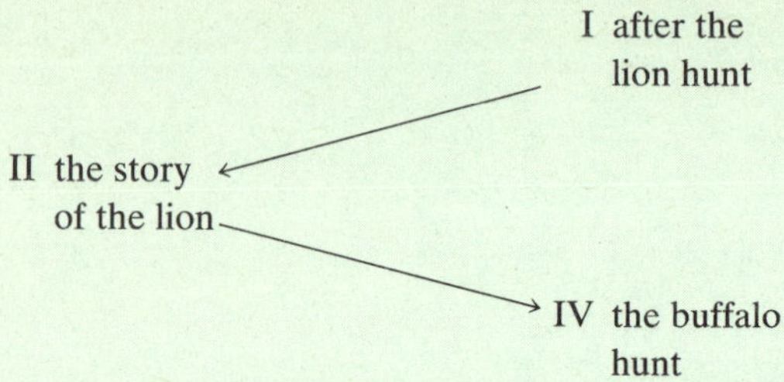

Both in structure and meaning, episode II is thus at the story's centre. It is twice reflected, first in the events of the afternoon and the night after the hunt, second in the parallel of the buffalo hunt. The first reflection is in the minds of the characters, it is cognitive and moral. The second reflection is different: not an explicit or insinuatingly allusive comment on Macomber's behaviour but straightforward dramatic action which both the characters in the story and the reader outside recognize as being similar to and different from the previous hunt.

Such a structural analysis is intended to show in an easy-to-grasp fashion how this story "works" and this should always be followed up and expanded by detailed reference to the story itself. As in classical rhetoric, the neat formal pattern is not an end in itself but a mnemonic support for the reader.[6]

It is noteworthy that the extended flashback (part 2) is preceded by a whole series of brief references to the hunt:

"You've got your lion" (**42** 12)
"Here's to the lion" (**42** 32; **43** 4)
"Let's not talk about the lion" (**43** 6)
"Got a damn fine lion" (**43** 25)
"I'm awfully sorry about that lion business" (**44** 29–30)
"You know in Africa no woman ..." (**45** 22–24)
"What importance is there to whether ..." (**46** 8–9)
"Tonight we'll have champagne for the lion" (**47** 19)
"I'd like to clear away that lion business" (**48** 14)

These references, in which bits of information slowly emerge, serve to whet the reader's appetite to hear the full story. They create narrative tension. At the same time, they make the reader realize how each of the three characters is trying to find a way of talking about what happened on the hunt.

6 Cf. Leech 1969, p. 67: "Linguistic parallelism is very often connected with rhetorical emphasis and memorability."

Macomber is trying to regain his poise and nursing his wounded ego, Margot shooting off poisoned barbs at her husband while just avoiding an overt quarrel in front of a stranger. In the case of Wilson the difference between what he thinks and what he says is greatest – more than the others he is restrained by the conventions of politeness.

This brings us to the familiar subject of knowing versus saying that has been touched on in the discussion of each of the previous stories. In the first part of the story it is a matter of not saying what everyone knows, everyone except the reader, that is. In the final part, from **57** 34 onwards, there is a growing tendency to try to say what one knows. The turning-point is situated half-way through the story in the scene where Margot returns to the Macombers' tent after inflicting on her husband what she doubtless regards as the fitting humiliation for a coward. In emphatic repetition she refuses to talk with Macomber: "But please let's not talk, darling" (**58** 19, and repeated 24, 30 and 32). But Macomber replies: "I'm going to talk" (**58** 33). Macomber is taking the decisive step here, just before the scene switches to daylight, to being honest and using language not to hide the truth but to say what is difficult and painful and honestly felt.

That the use of language should again be the subject of a unit is justified by its thematic importance and by its relevance for EFL readers. Thus in any of a number of passages the students can be asked to list and interpret the various deictic words, pro-forms and periphrastic expressions. The principle is established in the very first sentence: "... pretending that nothing had happened" (**41** 2). The obvious implication is that something *has* happened – only what? The implication is less obvious in a passage like the following in which Macomber reflects about "it":

> "... it was not all over. It was neither all over nor was it beginning. It was there exactly as it happened with some parts of it indelibly emphasized and he was miserably ashamed at it. But more than shame he felt cold hollow fear in him. The fear was still there like a cold slimy hollow in all the emptiness where once his confidence had been and it made him feel sick. It was still there with him now.
>
> It had started the night before when he had wakened and heard the lion roaring somewhere up along the river. It was a deep sound ..." (**48** 22–29)

Macomber is quite literally attempting to come to terms with his experience and his helplessness is reflected in the vagueness and changing reference of the repeated "it". In a later passage "it" ostensibly refers to one and the same thing, but because each of the speakers means something different they do not understand each other; during the buffalo hunt this exchange between Macomber and his wife occurs:

> "Wasn't it marvellous, Margot?"
> "I hated it."
> "Why?"
> "I hated it," she said bitterly. "I loathed it."
> "... It was pure excitement." (**65** 34–40)

Though they are both talking about the buffalo hunt, they have experienced it quite differently. For Macomber "it" means the "elation" of successful, virile hunting, for his wife "it" is the fright of a bumpy car ride and the chagrin of witnessing her husband's newly acquired fearlessness. Nick and Marjorie miscommunicated in exactly the same way. The EFL student as reader is called upon not only to say that and why the miscommunication takes place but also, and for language learning purposes more importantly, what it is that each speaker means. In this manner, the pervasive theme of knowing and saying, talking and not talking, can be made a thematic focus of interpretation and give rise to productive language exercises.

Another important aspect of the story is the use of different perspectives. This is a matter of technique but also of epistemology – how can an author tell his story most effectively, and through whose consciousness does he view the action? Some of the events are reported in an objective and dramatic fashion, the narrator keeping well out of the story, but not assuming knowledge not available to an observer. Then there are passages of comment and evaluation from an omniscient narrator who can transcend time and place. Still deeper knowledge is passed on to the reader in the inside views of all the characters, even of the lion (**51** 25 – **52** 2 and **55** 18–29). Wilson is used as "a kind of observer-chorus"[7] to provide a seemingly reliable view of the other characters and to set up norms of behaviour. This mixture of types of narration can be exploited in a course which aims to introduce students to the various ways of telling a story. But it can also be confusing. It is therefore suggested that teachers draw their students' attention to some of the more noticeable instances of narrative types and not attempt a detailed analysis. Any formal analysis must of course lead to the question of purpose and effect: Why did Hemingway choose to use objective report and inside views in alternation? Is the mixture of types a weakness or does it contribute to the story's meaning? A special problem is posed by the fact that part of the drama acted out between the figures is not expressed in audible speech but is given as thoughts and visual perceptions

---

7 R.S. Crane, "Ernest Hemingway: 'The Short Happy Life of Francis Macomber'," in: *The Idea of the Humanities and Other Essays, Critical and Historical,* Vol. 2, Chicago and London 1967, p. 325.

leading to thoughts. This is especially the case with Wilson, as the following example, a double spread in the pupils' book, will show:

44 10–11 Wilson could tell that the boys knew all about it now.
25 Then he felt embarrassed at asking it.
27 This was no better. "Good God", he thought. "I am a diplomat, aren't I?"
33–35 He had not expected this ...
45 4–13 He had decided now ...
15–17 Wilson noted ...
19–21 So what could he do, Wilson thought ...
25–26 Now what in hell ..., Wilson wondered.
28–29 He had a pleasant smile [Wilson thought] ...
32–36 Perhaps he had been wrong. This was certainly ...

This is a very mixed bag of inside views – report, thought as direct speech and thought as free indirect speech[8]. Often one cannot tell whether the descriptions and value judgements are by Wilson or by the omniscient off-scene narrator, and therefore one cannot be sure how reliable they are (e.g. **45** 28–29). Although this technique of inside views serves to put the reader in the privileged position of knowing more than any of the characters in the story, it does not save him the trouble of forming his own value judgements. Take the following example:

> "I bolted like a rabbit," Macomber said.
> Now what in hell were you going to do about a man who talked like that, Wilson wondered. (**45** 24–26)

What does "like that" mean? We are not told, so we have to find out for ourselves, and that means rewording Wilson's thoughts. Does he mean "like a coward" or "stupidly" or "truthfully"? A reader who opts for one of these or for any other rephrasing is interpreting the words of the text, but on the basis of his own, individual real-life experience. The reader's understanding is thus formed by criteria found in the text itself and by private experience. Any particular rewording, based on both, needs to be accounted for and discussed in class, i.e. a student will explain to his classmates why he thinks "like that" means "stupidly". The rewording and the justification both lead to language production. All instances of indetermi-

8 Cf. Geoffrey N. Leech and Michael H. Short, *Style in Fiction: A Linguistic Introduction to English Fictional Prose,* London 1981, pp. 325f. The German equivalent would be "erlebte Rede."

nate meaning in the text – pro-forms, deictic words, ellipses, periphrases and euphemisms – and the inclusion of personal experience and opinion have this effect. Suggestions on how to exploit them are made in the *Teaching Notes* (pp. 149ff.).

The Hero and the Code

Any discussion of Hemingway's fiction inevitably leads to the question of how a particular course of action or kind of behaviour may be justified. A man's life and the actions of which it is composed are represented fictionally in the action of a story or novel. The large task of defining the meaning of a man's life is concentrated and brought within a comprehensible compass in a short story when meaning is assigned to a hero's actions. A hero, in this sense, is a character subjected to particular scrutiny, so to speak under a magnifying glass.

It is something of a commonplace in Hemingway criticism that there are two kinds of hero in his work, one dependent on the other. The first is what is known as the "exemplary" or "code hero".[9] This is a comparatively mature and static figure who has undergone defeat and disillusionment and who has acquired skills and knowledge. This double experience enables him to exert control over himself and to maintain under duress the dignity essential to manhood. The code hero is thus, from the reader's point of view, the spokesman of certain virtues and standards, and, from the point of view of characters like Nick Adams, a model to be emulated. Nick is the prototype of the second kind of hero, the "apprentice", just as Robert Wilson, in the present selection, is the most obvious code hero.

The Nick Adams figures – and they include Harold Krebs, the 3rd Roman Soldier and Francis Macomber – characteristically undergo a development which centers on an experience of initiation of some kind. They are the real heroes, the centres of plot and theme. The apprentice heroes are shown as wounded in body or mind, frequently in both. Their knowledge of the world is imperfect (it is perfect only in a very restricted sphere) and their ability to express themselves is far less developed than their sharpened awareness of loss or mortality requires. All of Hemingway's apprentice heroes try to dull the pain of their wounds by some kind of

9 Young 1952, especially chapter 2 on "The Hero and the Code"; Earl Rovit, *Ernest Hemingway,* New York 1963, chapter 5; Waldhorn 1972, chapter 2 on "The World, the Hero and the Code."

escapism – drink, sex, day-dreaming, make-believe, gambling or actual flight.

Neither type of hero is perfect. The code hero succeeds in living according to a set of standards, but these are neither comprehensive nor pure. Wilson, for example, compromises: though he despises his safari customers, yet "their standards were his standards as long as they were hiring him" (**61** 14–15). But he does not compromise in the one matter that is essential to him: his professional honour. The text of the story goes on: "They were his standards in all except the shooting. He had his own standards about the killing and they could live up to them or get someone else to hunt for them. He knew, too, that they all respected him for this" (**61** 16–18). Wilson consequently rejects all of Macomber's attempts (partly motivated by lack of knowledge, partly by cowardice) to break or evade the rules of hunting (**53** 20 – **54** 16).

A more muted version of the code hero is Captain Paravicini in "A Way You'll Never Be". Waldhorn's definition seems to fit him well: "The code does not ask that a hero be fearless ... But it insists that he discipline and control his dread and, above all, that he behave with unobtrusive though unmistakeable dignity."[10] Not all the stories feature the code hero or give him prominence: there is none in "The End of Something" or in "Soldier's Home". In "Today Is Friday" it is of course Christ who embodies the code, but he inevitably remains off-stage.

It is noteworthy that the "apprentice" hero never achieves the assured status of the code hero: "The Hemingway hero, although he greatly admires this code, is not able to live by it. He is too tortured, too thoughtful, too perplexed for that."[11] The short stories consequently focus on the discrepancy between desire and performance, feeling and knowledge, knowing and saying, and defer any solution till after the narrative, or, in the case of Francis Macomber, cancel it out the very moment it is achieved. Cleanth Brooks concludes: "The Hemingway hero ... is doomed to defeat, but he insists upon being defeated on his own terms. There is the matter of the point of honor. For a final success is impossible – it is as a quixotic gesture that the hero makes his choice of acting one way rather than another. It is a mere gesture but it has its importance in that it proclaims him to be a man and not a mere automaton."[12]

---

10 Waldhorn 1972, p. 26.

11 Young 1952, p. 40.

12 Cleanth Brooks, *The Hidden God: Studies in Hemingway, Faulkner, Yeats, Eliot, and Warren,* New Haven and London 1963, pp. 10–11.

Supplementary Text

The supplementary text "Shootism versus Sport" is an article written for the magazine *Esquire* in 1934. It represents Hemingway, the journalist. It displays a number of similarities to "The Short Happy Life of Francis Macomber" but also significant differences. They are both based on Hemingway's 1933–34 safari, both are about hunting lions. Both distinguish between the wrong way to hunt and the right way, in particular as regards the use of a motor car to cover distances, to get close to the game and to shoot from. The journalistic text clearly aims to provide information for laymen readers and to convince them of the importance of the distinction between "shootism" (unfairly "murdering" a lion) and sport (keeping to the rules). One wonders what Hemingway's purpose was in making such a distinction. Did he feel compelled to justify a blood sport for which many of his readers may not have felt much sympathy, or did he want to prevent "shootists" back home from bragging about their unfairly gained trophies? The passage describing the killed lion (**73** 1–5) suggests that he had more sympathy for the animals than for the American tourist hunters. It is noticeable that there is no direct justification for hunting in the fictional text – what Hemingway wants to justify, to work out and demonstrate, is the much wider matter of the standards according to which one acts, i.e. the norms that direct Wilson's behaviour and which Macomber first contravenes and then begins to learn. So a comparison of the two texts shows how a factual description of hunting becomes a text in which hunting is a metaphor for acting well, hunting honestly and fearlessly for living happily. Fishing is a metaphor in the same way, so that Hemingway's code can be seen as a "sports-code morality" in which "the best fisherman is the one who plays the fish according to the rules which impose the highest degree of challenge on the fisherman without cancelling out his chances for success."[13]

A further point about the *Esquire* text is instructive. In the long middle section, from about **71** 19 on to **73** 5, the pronoun "you" is no longer impersonal (as in the preceding passage) but directly addresses the reader and so puts him into a "let's suppose you were in Africa on a lion hunt" position. Hemingway has here produced a kind of semi-fiction, an impression confirmed by the dialogue between the white hunter (anonymous) and the "you" (absent) that follows. Biography is worked up into journalism, journalism into fiction.

---

13 Rovit 1963, p. 108.

First Unit: Finding Out What Happened

A good way of preparing for work on "The Short Happy Life of Francis Macomber" is to have the students read the "Shootism versus Sport" article (**70–73**) as homework. It serves to introduce them to the theme of fair hunting and it provides a first rehearsal of some of the vocabulary. From there on, two alternative procedures are suggested:

Alternative A

Since this story is considerably longer than any of the others in this collection, the students can be asked to read it in sections. The work in class will then follow these sections:

1. **41** 1 – **48** 27 = 8 pages
2. **48** 28 – **58** 34 = 10 pages
3. **58** 35 – **70** 10 = 12 pages

The First to Third Units that follow refer to these three sections. The Fourth Unit aims at a general evaluation of the themes of the story, and the Fifth Unit deals with the concept of heroism in this and the other texts.

Alternative B

Because of its length, "The Short Happy Life" is a good opportunity to practise extensive reading. For this the students will be asked to concentrate on the main events and the differentiation of the three main characters. No vocabulary work beyond the basic annotations provided at the foot of each page is called for (cf. the explanations on p. 103). In weaker classes it will be perfectly acceptable to have the complete story read in German first (in *Schnee auf dem Kilimandscharo,* rororo 413) as long as all further work on the text is done in English and refers to the English text. If the complete text is read prior to the first classroom discussion, work should start with the Fourth Unit, followed by Units 1–3 and 5, adapting them where necessary.

Hemingway's way of telling "the story of the lion" is calculated to arouse the reader's curiosity. He does this through the abrupt beginning, by frequent references to un-narrated past time and through statements which hint at earlier events. The reader keeps having to ask himself "why?". The teacher's job would be to direct his students' attention to one example and then ask the class to find similar passages and to answer the questions they raise. As this reconstruction of previous events takes place, the reader comes to realize that the characters often speak in generalizations, euphemisms, half-truths and untruths. These also require "spelling out" or "putting right" by the reader.

1. *As you read the first two pages of this story, what do you find yourself wanting to know about previous events? List some passages that make you curious (like Margot* **42** *33 and Macomber's personal boy* **44** *12) and say what you think they imply.*

Examples:

41 2 "pretending that nothing had happened"
– Something must have happened.

42 5–6 "The gun-bearers had taken no part in the demonstration."
– Why not? Has something happened which is beneath their dignity, but not beneath the cook's, etc.?

42 8–9 She did not speak to him ..."
– Why not? What has he done?

42 22 "Wilson ... she knew she had never truly seen before."
– What has Wilson done to appear different to Mrs Macomber?

2. *Not all the characters are telling the truth or being frank. Find some instances of this in the first section. Say, as far as you can judge up to this point, what the truth in each case might be.*

Examples:

43 32–33 "Women upset ... Amounts to nothing."
– It does amount to something. Margot is not upset without reason. She is ashamed of her husband's cowardice and of the humiliation he has caused her.

44 2 "Nothing to it anyway."
– "It" means Macomber's running away from the lion (cf. **45** 24). It is a serious matter; Macomber's cowardice cannot be undone by Wilson politely and generously pretending it isn't.

44 5 "Nothing ... All nonsense."
– This is not true. Macomber is honestly grateful – after all, Wilson has saved his life.

44 26–27 "We all take a beating every day, you know, one way or another."
– This is an ambiguous generalization, intended by Wilson to gloss over Macomber's weakness, but understood by everyone as a quasi-proverbial hyperbolical metaphor for the inevitability of defeat. Though literally not true, it may be true in a wider sense, like "no one can win all the time".

45 22–23 "You know in Africa no woman ever misses her lion and no white man ever bolts."
– This is a polite fiction raised to a principle. Literally it is not true, but no woman will ever admit to missing the lion she has tried to hit and no man will ever admit that he has run away.

Further examples are Margot Macomber's ironies (**46** 5–6, 8–10 and **47** 21). By contrast, the subject of telling the truth can be discussed: a) the way Wilson recognizes the truth about Macomber and about Margot, but does not voice it; b) Macomber's honesty towards himself (especially **48** 22–27) and his attempts to be frank towards Wilson (e.g. **48** 14–18).

Second Unit: Why It Happened That Way

As pointed out above (pp. 140–142), the story of what happened that morning is the structural centre or pivot of the tale. The fact that it is narrated as a detailed flashback after we already know the broad outline affects what we pay attention to: we are not only interested in the details of what happened but above all in why it happened that way.

1. *Tell the story of the lion hunt briefly in your own words.*
This can be done as an oral exercise in class, or as written homework. In Unit 4 the students will be asked to comment on published summaries of the whole story. The main point for discussion and comparison will be to what extent the students' summaries manage to account for Macomber's flight. This is taken up in the following questions.

2. *What are the things or events that Francis Macomber is afraid of?*
Before the hunt:
- the roaring of the lion during the night (**48** 28 – **49** 2);
- Macomber's lack of confidence in his ability to shoot the lion (**49** 14–20);
- the prospect of having to confront the lion (cf. the Somali proverb **48** 36) at close range (**49** 21–28).

During the hunt:
- the sight of the lion (**51** 12–16);
- having to get down off the jeep (**51** 19–23);
- making a fool of himself (**52** 22).

After shooting the lion:
- having to go into the bush after the wounded lion (**52** 31 – **54** 18);
- wanting to admit to Wilson that he is afraid (**54** 34–36).

It is obvious to any reader that Macomber is afraid, less obvious what exactly causes his fear. Now our main interest in the spectacle of a man's fear should not be merely sensational but should ask what his consciousness of himself as a coward is. In other words: does Macomber recognize all the causes of his fear? What are the ones that he doesn't recognize, and why do they remain obscure to him (though perhaps he will recognize them later)? The teacher can introduce this extension of the topic linguistically by presenting the article "angst" as defined in various dictionaries, e.g. *ALD,* or the following from a popular dictionary of philosophy:

> **Angst.** (*German for:* anxiety, anguish.) In existentialist philosophy, the dread occasioned by man's realization that his existence is open towards an undetermined future, the emptiness of which must be filled by his freely chosen actions. Anxiety characterizes the human state, which entails constant confrontation with possibility and the need for decision, with the concomitant burden of responsibility.
> (Antony Flew, ed., *A Dictionary of Philosophy,* London ²1984 (Pan)).

For most students it will be a surprise to find that a German word (which figures prominently in current political debate on the arms race, 3rd world poverty etc.) should be an item of the English lexicon. Defining the term helps to clarify that Macomber's fear of the lion is, at bottom, not mere cowardice; it is the expression of an uncomprehended anxiety, mainly about his own status or value. He is anxious whether he can live up to the image of the kind of man he would like to be, or his wife would like him to be. This is made quite clear in an unobtrusive detail later in the story. Macomber, disgusted with himself and consequently furious at everyone and everything, is warned by Wilson to mind his words because "there's a boy at table that understands a little English" and retorts "The hell with him" (**59** 32–34). The retort would normally be taken to mean "I don't care if he understands", but it is really only a poor attempt at hiding that he does indeed care very much. One is reminded of Nick's traumatic neurosis in "A Way You'll Never Be". Once the students realize that self-knowledge is involved in Macomber's fear, the following assignment can be tackled.

3. *Make a list of the things that Macomber does not know during and after the hunt. What do these tell you about him?*
First, there is a whole series of questions that betray Macomber's lack of knowledge:
- "How far is he?" (**51** 17)
- "Why not shoot from where I am?" (**51** 19)
- "What do you mean?" (**52** 28)
- "Why is it bad?" (**52** 33)
- "What do we do?" (**53** 16)
- "Can't we set the grass on fire?" (**53** 20)
- "What about the gun bearers?" (**53** 30)
- "Why not leave him there?" (**54** 3)

– “Why not just leave him?” (**54** 9)
– “Why not?” (**54** 13)

Then we are informed by the narrator of what is going on in Macomber’s mind:
– “Macomber had not thought how the lion felt ...” (**52** 3)
– “He could not know that Wilson was furious ...” (**54** 36–38)
– “Macomber did not know how the lion had felt ...” (**56** 33 – **57** 5)

The last passage in this list is complex and leads on to question 4. Another passage, not so easy to identify because it is a familiar colloquialism, is **55** 34–36, “The next thing he knew ...”, suggesting that Macomber does not know what happened to him as he took flight. The meaning of all this evidence can be summarized by saying that Macomber has not learnt the laws of hunting yet. He is an apprentice, one who has not undergone the necessary initiation. Put like this, Macomber is not so much a coward as an innocent.

4. *Describe the relationship between Macomber and his wife during the lion-hunt episode. To what extent does it help to explain Macomber’s behaviour?*
The first point to make is that Macomber is entirely on his own: “There was no one to tell he was afraid, nor to be afraid with him ...” (**48** 32–33). Margot Macomber does not share his problems and so does not help to make them more bearable. From such an estrangement her kissing Wilson (**56** 22–23) and her adultery follow as inevitable next steps.

Then there is the conversation at the breakfast table. Margot shows no understanding for her husband’s nervousness and her reaction to the lion’s roaring is in mocking contrast to his (**49** 36 – **50** 24). This parallels their dialogue after the buffalo hunt (**65** 34–40; discussed above p. 144). To Macomber, a question like “You’re not afraid, are you?” (**50** 12) is nothing but a taunt, and the following “You’ll kill him marvellously” bitter irony. His wife makes fun of him and humiliates him whenever she can.

Their relationship is summarized at the end of the flashback. This too stresses what Macomber does not know: “He did not know how his wife felt except that she was through with him” (**57** 4–5), and immediately after that: “he knew she would not leave him ever now. That was one of the few things he really knew.” The Macombers know nasty things about each other. They do not know each other in love. Such a positive standard is missing in their relationship. The dialogue following Margot’s return from Wilson’s tent confirms this (**58** 6–34).

So, in part at least, Macomber's cowardice can be explained by his loneliness and by his wife's lack of sympathy.

The discussion of the relationship between the Macombers can be extended to include part F (**58** 35 – **60** 21).

Third Unit: Macomber's Conversion

The first two units, finding out what happened and why, are the necessary steps towards understanding the change that Macomber undergoes during the buffalo hunt. Is it Macomber's character that is transformed, and if so, is that transformation sufficiently accounted for in the story? Or is Macomber's "manly" or "heroic" behaviour a flash in the pan due to his momentary feelings of hate and anger, and will he revert to his habitual cowardice once his anger has subsided? It is not quite clear, either, when the change in Macomber takes place – is it during the buffalo hunt, or directly afterwards, or when they go into the brush to finish off the wounded beast? The explicit answer given in the text is unsatisfactory: "It had taken a strange chance of hunting, a sudden precipitation into action without opportunity for worrying beforehand, to bring this about with Macomber, but regardless of how it happened it had most certainly happened" (**66** 18–21). This is presumably Wilson's unreliable point of view and it certainly begs more questions than it answers. Perhaps the best way of describing Macomber's change is to see it as a gradual development, a step-by-step conversion to manhood. To call it a conversion is to suggest that Macomber can in this respect be compared to the 3rd Roman soldier in "Today Is Friday".

1. *Compare the following summaries. How do they describe or explain Macomber's change?*
2. *What account do the summaries give of Margot's final rifle-shot? How would* you *explain her action?*

a) Max J. Herzberg, *The Reader's Encyclopedia of American Literature,* London and New York 1962 (Methuen).
"... the Macombers, an American couple, are on a safari in Africa with the Englishman Wilson as their guide. When confronted with a mad, wounded lion, Macomber proves himself a coward, is saved by Wilson, and earns his wife's utter contempt. On the next hunting expedition, Macomber feels a gathering strength and his wife, who has always found gratification in his weakness, is suddenly frightened by this new Macomber. His second chance comes with a wild buffalo. Cowardice vanishes and as he heroically tries to

fell the onrushing beast, a bullet fired by his wife misses the buffalo and kills Macomber."

b) Almut von Wullfen, in: *Kindlers Literaturlexikon,* Bd. VI. "Doch während der Büffeljagd am nächsten Morgen fällt die Angst plötzlich wie ein Tuch von Macomber ab. In kühler Selbstbeherrschung legt er auf einen angeschossenen Büffel an, der blindwütig auf ihn zurast. In diesem Augenblick trifft ihn die Kugel, die seine Frau dem Anschein nach auf das angreifende Tier abgefeuert hat. Wilson deckt die psychologischen Hintergründe dieses 'Unfalls' auf: In der blitzartigen Erkenntnis, daß der durch seinen Todesmut mündig und glücklich gewordene Macomber sie verlassen würde, hat Margaret ihn getötet."

c) Leo Gurko, *Ernest Hemingway and the Pursuit of Heroism,* New York 1968, p. 197.
"... The next day, angry, bitter, and ashamed, but in some curious way purged of his fear, Macomber faces up to the wounded buffalo that charges him in a swift unexpected rush. His new-found courage releases him into happiness, but his happy life proves short, scarcely more than two seconds, for his wife, unable to bear the prospect of her husband's bravery, fires a bullet into his brain."

Simply placing these different summaries side by side can show the students that it is perfectly legitimate and natural to come to different conclusions about what happens in a story and how much more likely still differing evaluations are. The students can then be asked to express and justify their preference for any one summary. There should be no attempt to try to agree on a harmonious "final" version.

At this point it may be useful to provide a simple visualized summary of the story as a framework for previous and subsequent discussion of detail. The procedure, which is best chalked step by step on the blackboard, is simply to ask "Who hunts whom?". In the first hunt this can be represented thus:

①

The hunter (H) pursues his game (G, in this case the lion). The lion first flees but then attacks and puts the aggressor to flight. The diagram now becomes:

(1a)

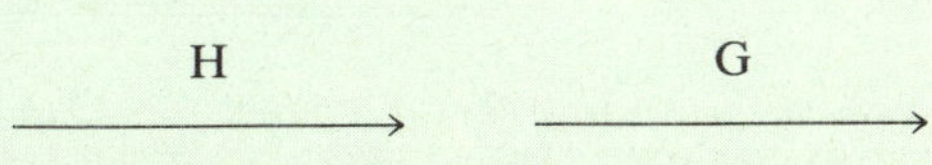

Through outside intervention (by Wilson) the lion, who is really the victor, is killed:

(1b)

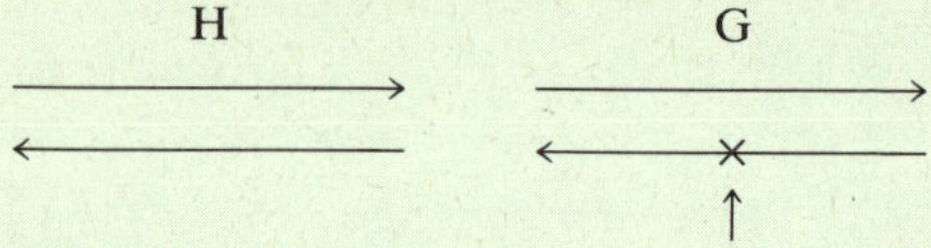

The second hunt is less complicated, representing the normal outcome: the impala are hunted, they flee and are killed:

②

In the third hunt we have the same initial situation:

③

As in ①, the buffalo counters the attack, but this time the hunter stands and kills the buffalo himself, without help from outside:

(3a)

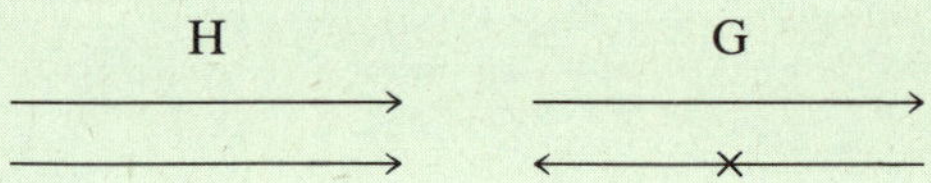

But then, again as in ①, the real victor of the contest is slain from outside:

(3b)

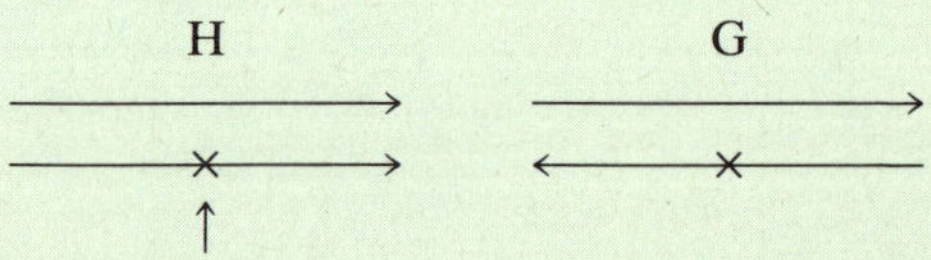

So finally there are three comparable diagrams on the blackboard, the normal contest in the middle, and the parallel yet contrasting contests on the left and right. The third hunt echoes the first in its essential element: the unmerited death of the victor. The implication is that there is no way the victor can finally win or escape death – a basic conviction of Hemingway's (cf. the title of his collection of stories *Winner Take Nothing*). The price of courage is death.

3. *Interpret and comment on the following reading of Macomber's conversion: it is Cleanth Brooks' view that Macomber is an exemplar of Christian courage.*

"If one turns the other cheek because he is afraid not to turn it, he is not exhibiting Christianity. ... The specifically Christian virtue is exercised only by the man who turns his cheek though he is not in the least afraid. Hemingway's emphasis upon courage ... [is] a first step in moving back toward the Christian virtues. Hemingway, of course, stops short of the domain of Christianity proper, but he does see that the man who lacks courage, a mere slave to his fears, is not truly free and not truly human."[14]

The quote from Brooks is best presented in written form, via transparency or as a handout.The teacher can preface this rather more difficult assignment by giving his class the Biblical text alluded to by Brooks:

Matthew 5:39: "But I say to you, do not resist one who is evil. But if any one strikes you on the right cheek, turn to him the other also." Also Luke 6:27–31: "But I say to you that hear, Love your enemies, do good to those who hate you, bless those who curse you, pray for those who abuse you. To him who strikes you on the cheek, offer the other also; and from him who takes away your coat do not withhold even your shirt. Give to everyone who begs from you; and of him who takes away your goods do not ask them again. And as you wish that men would do to you, do so to them." *(Revised Standard Version)*

The story contains no direct references to Christian virtues. In Brooks' view, courage and freedom are the key values which define such virtue. If courage is taken to mean loss of fear then both in Macomber's self-estimate and in Wilson's judgement the American finally becomes courageous. The important part of Brooks' definition is not mere fearlessness but consciously accepting a risk or danger and consciously being not afraid. It is therefore because Macomber acts with growing consciousness that one can describe his change as a conversion. However, the reader's knowledge of Macomber reaches further than Macomber's self-knowledge: what is "a wild unreasonable happiness" (**65** 31) to Macomber is perhaps unexpected, but not unreasonable to the reader.

Fourth Unit: The Relation of Saying and Doing

The question of language has been variously discussed in connection with the other stories in this reader. The guiding principle of this approach was to connect as closely as possible the analysis of linguistic features with language production. The reader's language production, speaking and writ-

14 Brooks 1963, pp. 14–15.

ing, is characteristically sparked off by those features of the text in which imperfect or incomplete communication takes place. They are also stimulated by the processes of mental and thus linguistic development portrayed in the hero. Thus, the first three units have attempted to work out how Macomber's lack of knowledge gradually gives way to a measure of awareness. We now turn to the question of how Macomber finds words for the change that he has undergone, and then to the attitudes that Wilson and Margot, and Macomber himself, display towards speaking about the change. The debate is finally about the relative value of deeds and words – a debate familiar to all of us.

1. *Check part Gb of the story (**64** 23 – **67** 27) for passages which have for their subject Macomber's attempt to find words for his experience. What do these passages tell you about the nature of his change?*

65 33–34 "By God, that was a chase ..."
38–40 "You know I don't think ..."
66 3–4 "You know something ..."
8–9 "You know I'd like to try ..."
67 4–5 "Do you have that feeling ..."
9 "But you *have* ..."
17–18 "If you don't know what we're talking about ..."

The first point to make is that Macomber is struck dumb for quite a while after the hunt is over. From **63** 8 to **65** 30 he says almost nothing about his own state of mind, but from then on grows gradually more voluble and explicit. Second point: the repetitiveness of his utterances is most noticeable when they are copied out one underneath the other, as above. In each of them Macomber is voicing an appeal, begging for confirmation. In the last utterance (**67** 17–18), however, he asserts himself, i.e. he intends to exclude Margot from the communion achieved with Wilson. Saying this is to make the third point: Macomber has grown more and more sure of himself. He has found simple words for his feelings, they sound authentic. The opposition to Margot is again telling: when she uses the words "awfully brave" to mock her husband he can honestly, unironically take up the expression in its literal meaning. The teacher may point out the literal meaning of "awe-full" or have it looked up.

2. *How does Wilson react to Macomber's "self-exploration"* (**67** 5)? *What do his comments and reported thoughts tell you about him?*
His reaction is mixed. He is surprised at the change in Macomber (**65** 22–23) into speaking on a subject he is normally silent about. His comments (**66**

1–2, 10–14) are honest and the staccato syntax of his thoughts (**66** 21–32) and further statements (**67** 6–8, 10–12) suggest that he is not in the habit of talking about anything much except the technicalities of hunting (and in this he resembles the Nick of "The End of Something" and of "A Way You'll Never Be"). They also make quite clear that he prefers deeds to words (confirmed by **48** 16–17) and so his quoting Shakespeare is all the more astonishing. But Wilson doesn't reject Macomber's self-analysis except to point out that it "doesn't do to talk too much about [it]" (**67** 10). He accepts Macomber's change and even admires him for it.

3. *How does Margot react? Compare her actions and her words.*
She is more concerned with herself than with understanding her husband. Instead of admiring the positive change in Macomber, she fears the negative change that it implies for her. One can assume that she anticipates that her husband would in the future become independent of her, or even leave her, just as Wilson suggests at the end of the story (**69** 28–29). As Macomber shakes off his fear, Margot falls prey to hers (**63** 28; **65** 25–26). A simple diagram can help to show this:

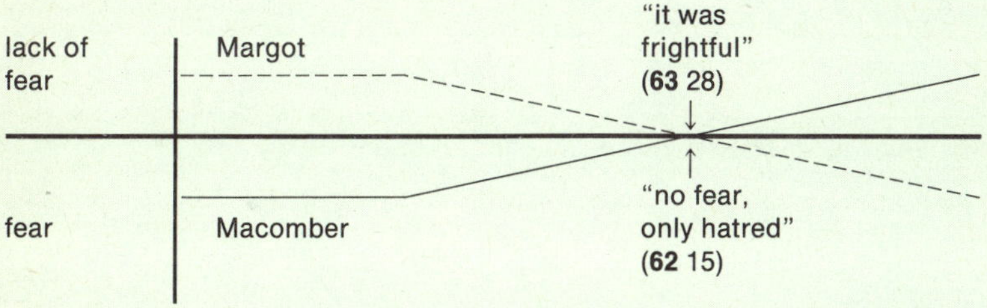

In self-protection, Margot scoffs at the change she is powerless to prevent (**67** 13–14, 19–23). Her words are intended to hide both her real feelings and her inability to act. This is neatly shown in the way she corrects the give-away "it was frightful" into "it was frightfully exciting" (**63** 33). All she can do now is to wait and watch, ready to pounce, like a wild animal driven into a corner (**66** 5; **66** 33 – **67** 3; **68** 23–24).

This brings the discussion to the way the story ends. The details discussed above are only really understood at a second reading of the story. Reading the story for the first time and naturally concentrating on what happens next Margot Macomber's final deed comes as a surprise. Yet it is carefully prepared by Hemingway and perhaps premeditated by Margot herself.

4. *Does the ending of the story come as a surprise to you? Do you think the killing is accidental or intentional?*

- Yes, the ending is surprising. Towards the end of the story one is just beginning to understand Macomber's change. Suddenly and needlessly he is shot dead. One can't tell for sure whether this is an accident or not.
- Wilson clearly thinks Margot killed her husband on purpose. Calling it an accident (**69** 31) is just irony, and the sarcastic question "Why didn't you poison him?" mocks her for not having killed him in the "conventional" stealthy feminine manner.
- The ending is a bit of a shock but not really a surprise. There are a number of suggestions that something is going to happen, e.g.

  60 20–21 Wilson imagines himself as the possible victim of Macomber, but in his mind it is Margot that he makes responsible: "Women *are* a nuisance on a safari." The ending of the story confirms this.

  61 23 The fact that Mrs Macomber, when she joined Wilson in his double cot, "hadn't talked much" makes the hunter speculate about her: "What's in her heart God knows …".

  64 31 Margot hopes that her husband will prove himself a coward again. When this anticipation is disappointed and the reversal in Macomber's behaviour occurs it is reasonable to assume that there will be an attempt by Margot to do *something*.

Cf. also the passages mentioned under question 3.

Fifth Unit: The Hero and the Code

The teacher can either briefly introduce the distinctions made above on pp. 146–147 and then discuss with the class how they are realized in the story, or he can proceed inductively via the questions.

1. *What do Wilson's judgements of the Macombers tell you about his own standards?*

On Francis Macomber (**44–45**):
One must not be a coward like Macomber nor must one neglect the rules of

good form, as Macomber does when he asks Wilson not to tell others about the incident. One should not indulge in emotional talk, one should swallow an insult with dignity and not apologize unnecessarily. Instead of pretending, one should "make a good clean break" if one's basic standards are affected. If one has made a fool of oneself the only thing to do is to act differently in the future (i.e. deeds are better than words; cf. **45** 30–33).

On Margot (**46–47**):
Wilson mistakenly believes Margot to be "a hell of a fine woman" because she is "hard", i.e. self-controlled, and at the same time "seemed to understand, to realize, to be hurt for him and for herself and to know how things really stood" (**46** 27–28). This passage really summarizes Wilson's own ideals: pride, sympathy and understanding. But then he sees her for what she really is and rejects her vindictive hardness and cruelty, her basic egoism.

On standards (**61**):
Here Wilson distinguishes between his clients' standards, which he adopts for as long as he is financially dependent on them, and his own essential standards in hunting. For these latter he will accept no compromise, since his self-respect depends on maintaining them.

2. *What does Wilson mean by "this thing he had lived by"* (**66** 15)? *What is the "something" that grows in a man when he has cast off fear* (cf. **66** 30–31)?
These are two characteristic indeterminacies. All along the story has been providing the information and the clues needed to fill in these semantic blanks. No reading of the story is satisfactory which does not try to fill them in. "This thing he had lived by" refers to the quotation from Shakespeare. It is Wilson's central article of faith. A man who stoically accepts that death is inevitable and who is consequently not afraid can achieve an attitude or state of mind that we can call pride or dignity or happiness or ...

3. *To what extent can you sympathize with Macomber? In what respect do you like or dislike him?*
No "model answers" can be furnished here. The teacher can point out that one of the functions of the hero figure in a work of fiction is to allow the reader to sympathize with a flawed model figure. While the code hero (Wilson) provides the moral yardstick it is the apprentice hero who is more interesting, on whom the tension of "what will happen to him?" focuses. He is the figure in whom processes of learning and maturation are worked out and made comprehensible.

4. *What is the relationship between Wilson and Macomber? What is their function in the story?*

Wilson "code hero"	Macomber "Hemingway hero" "apprentice hero"
static	able to develop
fearless	must learn to overcome fear
strictly adheres to a set of rules, a "code" of behaviour	initially breaks these rules because of lack of knowledge
is in possession of a degree of wisdom	acquires this wisdom in the end
"mentor"	"apprentice"

For Further Study

1. As a final assignment a comparison of the protagonists in all the five stories in this collection is proposed. This could be set as written homework or for a short report to be made orally in class from notes.
2. Alternatively, and perhaps with greater motivational effect, the following text can be read to the class to bring the course to an end on a humorous note:

Ernest Hemingway

Ernest Hemingway began his writing career as a contributor to the Oak Park High School yearbook. About the same time he had the first faint indications of what later qualified him as the leader of the Hairy-Chested School of Writers. Subsequently he continued his journalistic career on a newspaper and then, when he had saved up enough to buy a trench coat, became a foreign correspondent.

Hairy-chested school

Always interested in sports, he is said to have worn boxing gloves while typing, which may account for an occasional blurred image. His most celebrated physical encounter was his bout with Max Eastman, who had intimated that Ernest wore a toupee on his chest. In addition to his prowess as a boxer, he was good at fishing and shooting, and brought back several mounted heads from Africa.

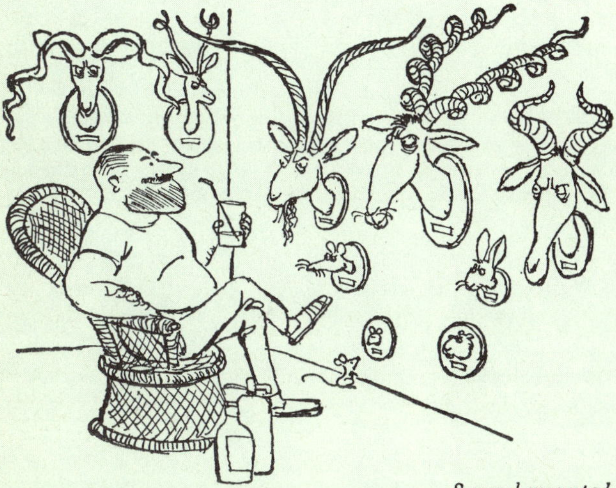

Several mounted heads

During World War I, Hemingway served with an ambulance unit in Italy. He was wounded and decorated with the Croce di Guerra and the Medaglia d'Argento al Valore Militare. Better than medals, because he always carried them with him, were several scars which made interesting conversation pieces. In the hospital, 237 pieces of shrapnel were removed from his legs, Hemingway keeping the tally on a clipboard. Not satisfied with these wounds, he also served as a correspondent in both the Spanish Civil War and World War II, in the latter gaining quite a reputation among our troops for keeping his canteen filled with cognac.

Hemingway had four wives,[1] always being in search of adventure and looking for "the real thing." Or perhaps it was just that he liked women young and vibrant, like the heroines in his books, and so kept trading them in for later models. Besides, unless they were considerably younger than he, it seemed a little ridiculous for them to call him "Papa."

...

Hemingway, who was influenced by Sherwood Anderson and Gertrude Stein, in turn influenced countless young writers who will doubtless influence still

1 One at a time.

others, and there is no telling when this will stop. Hemingway's greatest contribution has been in the economy of dialogue, which probably goes back to his early days when he didn't know where the next word was coming from. An example, from *The Sun Also Rises:*

"It's hot."
"Hot, my God!"
"Take off your hat."
"That's a good idea."

The reader will notice how Hemingway has got rid of the nonessentials and is moving toward that mastery of the writer's art which would permit him also to get rid of the essentials.

Richard Armour, *American Lit Relit: A short history of American literature for long-suffering students, for teachers who manage to keep one chapter ahead of the class, and for all those who, no longer being in school, can happily sink back into illiteracy,* ill. by Campbell Grant, New York 1964 (McGraw-Hill), pp. 150–154. Reprinted by permission.

"The Short Happy Life of Francis Macomber" was put into film in 1947 by United Artists as *The Macomber Affair,* directed by Z. Korda, and starring Gregory Peck (Macomber), Joan Bennett (Margot) and Robert Preston (Wilson). The film version can be compared with the story.

Additional Vocabulary

41 1 **fly** *here:* cloth roof – 8 **mess boy** servant responsible for serving drinks – 11 **What had I ought to give them?** *A.E. coll.* What ought I to give them? (cf. **43** 8)

42 23 **sandy** yellowish-red – **stubby** short – 25 **to groove** to form a line or fold – 26 **tunic** ['tju:nɪk] loose jacket, with a belt at the waist – 27 **loop** (Schlaufe) – 28 **slacks** comfortable, loose trousers – 30 **Stetson hat** hat with a wide brim – 31 **peg** (Pflock) – 35 **cropped** *here:* cut short

43 1 **court games** tennis, badminton, etc. – **big game** large animals, here fish like the marlin (Fächerfisch) that Hemingway himself loved to catch off Key West *(cf. the photo on p. 8)* – 19 **I say** *B.E.* (Hören Sie mal) – 32 **to upset** *used intransitively here in the sense of* to get upset easily

44 7 **acacia** [ə'keɪʃə] – **boulder-strewn** ['bəʊldə 'stru:n] covered with big rocks – 8 **stretch** area – 13 **to snap at s.o.** to speak to someone angrily – **blank** without expression – 20 **to raise a row** ['raʊ] to make a fuss, to complain

45 32 **flat** expressionless

46 1 **Memsahib** ['memsɑ:b] *Anglo-Indian:* lady – 19 **buff** *short for* buffalo – 29 **to enamel** [ɪ'næməl] (emaillieren)

47 6 **eland** ['i:lənd] kind of antelope – 17 **to tine** *rare* to stick (a fork in) – 35 **swale** [sweɪl] (Mulde) – 36 **orchard bush** area covered with orchard grass (Knäuelgras)

48 1 **impala** African antilope – 2 **ram** *syn.:* **buck** the male of certain animals – 3 **creditable** praiseworthy – 21 **cot** camp bed – **bar** barrier; *here:* net

49 35 **beggar** *slang:* fellow

50 18 **guttural** ['gʌtərəl] produced in the throat – 25 **big-bored** (großkalibrig) – 26 **Gibbs** ['gɪbz] – 27 **Springfield** two types of rifle – 28 **solids** *here:* solid bullets, as opposed to the usual hollow ones – 31 **racket** *slang:* noise – 34 **breech** (Verschlußöffnung) – 35 **to put the rifle on safety** (das Gewehr sichern)

51 2 **vulture** ['vʌltʃə] big bird which feeds on dead animals (Geier) – 3 **to plummet** to fall vertically – 5 **to lay up** to rest – 16 **to bulk** to appear large – 28 **to detach** to separate – 30 **slam** violent blow – 31 **grain** smallest unit of weight, 0.065 grams – 36 **froth** (Schaum)

52 1 **to crouch** to lie down, ready to spring up again – 6 **to sight (on)** (anvisieren) – 7 **junction** place where two parts meet – **trigger** (Abzug) – 19 **cocked** ready to fire (gespannt) – 20 **Wakamba = Kamba** a Bantu language of Kenya; **Wakamba** *means* member of the Kamba tribe – 23 **gut** belly – 37 **spoor** track or trail of a wild animal pursued as game

53 8 **Swahili** important Bantu language – 9 **bwana** *Swahili* master – 12 **to project** [prə'dʒekt] to stick out – 22 **beater** s.o. who makes a noise by beating on the ground, etc., to disturb an animal – 31 **shauri** *Swahili* advice; *here:* job, business

54 20 **to growl** [graʊl] to make a low warning sound – 22 **to back up** to support

55 5 **gloom** melancholy, unhappiness – 8 **canteen** *A.E.* water bottle – **to unbuckle** to unfasten – 10 **shoddy** of poor quality – **felt** (Filz) – 12 **to ripple** to move gently like waves on calm water – 16 **to twitch** to make short quick movements – 17 **tuft** bunch of hair – 21 **tawny** ['tɔ:nɪ] brownish yellow colour – 22 **hide** skin – 34 **to swish** to move with a soft hissing sound

56 3 **to blast** to explode – 4 **bulk** mass – 5 **clearing** open space – 28 **tendon** (Sehne) – 29 **bloating** *usually* **bloated** swelling; swollen – 35 **muzzle velocity** ['mʌzl vɪ'lɒsɪtɪ] speed with which a bullet leaves a gun

57 10 **salmon** ['sæmən] (Lachs) – **big-sea** i.e. big-sea fishing – 23 **disruption** separation – 24 **society columnist** ['kɒləmnɪst] journalist who writes about society events, scandals, famous people, etc. – 25 **ever-enduring** endless – 26 **In Darkest Africa** book by Sir Henry Morton Stanley (1841–1904) on his explorations in central Africa, published 1890 – 26 **the Martin Johnsons; Old Simba; Tembo** these and the other words in italics refer to the false picture of Africa drawn in sentimental Hollywood wild-life films by Martin E. Johnson (1884–1937) and his wife

58 4 **to pound** to beat heavily – 40 **topping** *B.E. coll.* excellent

59 4 **plaster** (Gips) – **I'm not a plaster saint** (ich bin doch kein Heiliger) – 24 **rot** *slang* nonsense – 32 **laddybuck** *coll.* young fellow – 33 **to wait (at table)** to serve

60 16 **woolly** *coll.* woollen sweater – 20 **notion** ['nəʊʃn] idea – 22 **to grind** *here:* to drive slowly and noisily – **pebble** small round stone – 23 **to angle** to move at an angle so as to minimize the gradient – 24 **to shovel** [ʌ] to dig with a shovel (schaufeln) – 25 **rolling country** (welliges Gelände) – 26 **dew** (Tau) – 28 **frond** leaf of a fern or certain type of bush – **verbena** [vɜ:'bi:nə] (Eisenkraut) – 29 **bracken** fern (Adlerfarn) – 33 **swamp** [swɒmp] (Sumpf) – 34 **they fed out into** as they fed they moved forward

61 6/7 **poor beggar/poor sod** *slang* poor fellow – 10 **clientele** [ˌkliən'tel] customers – 21 **grim** stern, very serious – 30 **wart-hog** (Warzenschwein)

62 2 **upswept** bent upwards – 3 **heads out** with their heads stretched forwards – 8 **scabby** (schorfig) – 11 **to jump (the road, the rails)** to leave suddenly – 12 **sparsely** ['spɑ:slɪ] thinly – 13 **nostril** openings in the nose – **muzzle** mouth of an animal (*and cf.* **56** 35) – 15 **to clamp on the brakes** *(verb with level stress)* to apply the brakes suddenly and firmly – 22 **to toss** to move restlessly from side to side or up and down – 28 **spout** (Fontäne)

63 6 **to deafen** ['defn] to make so much noise that one becomes unable to hear – **to stagger** to move unsteadily – 16 **to jerk** [dʒɜ:k] to make rapid, sudden movements – **to bellow** to roar – 31 **neat whisky** whisky without water added

64 16 **to put** *here:* to express

65 18 **to hell along** to race along "like hell" – 23 **ruddy** red, *here:* emphatic swear word, variation on "bloody"

66 12 William Shakespeare, *King Henry IV,* Part II, Act III, scene ii; An English friend of Hemingway's, E.E. Dorman-Smith, had copied out these lines for Hemingway while he was in Milan in 1918. – 18 **chance** *here:* coincidence – **precipitation** [prɪˌsɪpɪ'teɪʃn] hurrying

68 2 **Mannlicher** type of rifle; the name is perhaps intended as a pun on "männlicher" since Margot kills her husband with this rifle at the very moment when he has asserted his virility. – 6 **to thrust** to push – 9 **fancy** *here:* special, complicated – 17 **foliage** ['fəʊlɪɪdʒ] leaves – 34 **bloodshot** (blutunterlaufen) – 36 **slate** (Schiefer)

69 6 **a touch high** a little bit too high – 16 **to contort** to pull out of shape – 24 **tick** parasitic insect (Zecke)

70 3 **the lake** Lake Victoria – 7 **to be through** *here:* to have finished